DAY WALKS IN NEW ZEALAND
100 Great Tracks

For Tania

Sunrise on Aoraki/Mt Cook from Hooker Valley

DAY WALKS IN NEW ZEALAND
100 Great Tracks

Text and photographs by Shaun Barnett
Maps by Roger Smith, Geographx

craig potton publishing

ACKNOWLEDGEMENTS

I would like to thank a number of people who have been great walking companions: David Barnes, Angela Barnett, Grant Barnett, Rob Brown, Dave Chowdhury, Andy Dennis, Dave Hansford, Andrew Lynch, Ken MacIver, Chris Maclean, Geoff Norman, Darryn Pegram, Jock Phillips, Mark Stanton, Tania Stanton, Tom Stanton-Barnett, Lee Stanton-Barnett and Louise Thornley. A number of other people also provided help with advice, transport or accommodation, which was greatly appreciated: Rob Brown and Elise Bryant, Liz and Mike Sampson, Jason Roxburgh, Darryn Pegram and Rachel Bryce, Bruce Postill, Rob Hungerford, Ruth Hungerford and Simon Ashworth, Mark Stanton and Heather Mitchell, Alison Taylor and David Sinclair, David Barnes and Anne-Marie McIlroy, Viv Milne.

The DOC website (www.doc.govt.nz), as well as their brochures and information panels proved to be excellent sources of information. It goes without saying that any mistakes are mine alone: if you find a significant error, email or write to the publisher, as I would appreciate knowing about it for future editions.

Unless otherwise credited, all photos are by Shaun Barnett/Black Robin Photography.

First published in 2007 by Craig Potton Publishing

Craig Potton Publishing
98 Vickerman Street, PO Box 555, Nelson, New Zealand
www.craigpotton.co.nz

© Maps by Geographx

© Photography and text: Shaun Barnett and individual photographers

ISBN: 978-1-877333-67-5

Printed in China by Midas Printing International Ltd

Opposite *Tramper in the water-eroded limestone of Sawcut Gorge, Isolation Hill Scenic Reserve, Kaikoura*

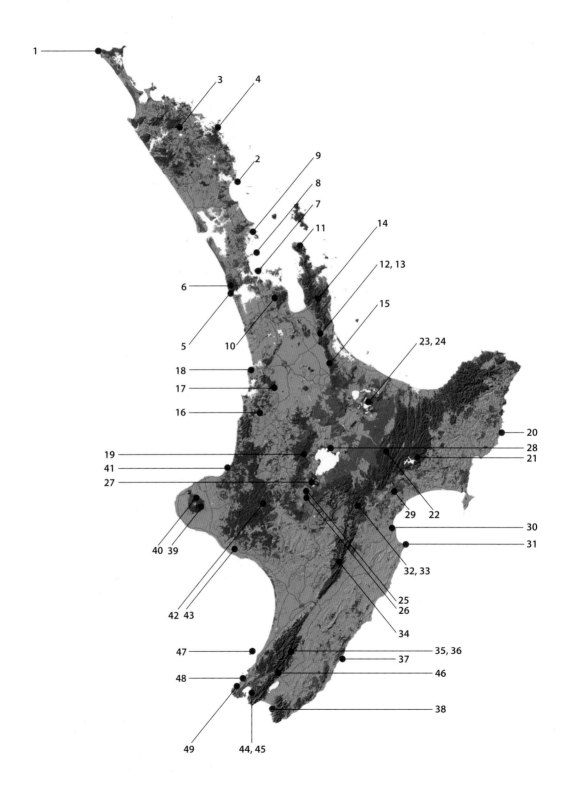

CONTENTS

Introduction   10

Northland   16
1   Cape Reinga Coastal Walkway

Bream Head Scenic Reserve, Whangarei   18
2   Te Whara Track

Puketi Forest, Northland   20
3   Waihoanga Gorge Kauri Walk

Whangamumu Scenic Reserve   21
4   Whangamumu Harbour, Bay of Islands

Waitakere Ranges Regional Park   22
5   Karekare–Pararaha
6   Montana Heritage Trail

Hauraki Gulf   26
7   Rangitoto Island

Hauraki Gulf   28
8   Tiritiri Matangi Island

Tawharanui Regional Park   30
9   Maori Bay Coast Walk

Hunua Ranges Regional Park   32
10   Hunua Falls & Cosseys Dam

Coromandel Peninsula   33
11   Coromandel Walkway

Coromandel   35
12   Kauri Loop Walk, Waitawheta Valley, Kaimai–Mamaku Forest Park
13   Karangahake Gorge Historic Walkway, Paeroa

Coromandel Forest Park   39
14   Kauaeranga Kauri Trail

Kaimai–Mamaku Forest Park   41
15   Wairere Falls

King Country   42
16   Tawarau Forest

Pirongia Forest Park   44
17   Mangakara Nature Walk & Ruapanae

Pirongia Forest Park   46
18   Te Toto Gorge & Mt Karioi

Pureora Forest Park   48
19   Mt Pureora

East Coast   49
20   Cook's Cove Walkway

Te Urewera National Park   50
21   Lake Waikareiti

Whirinaki Forest Park   52
22   Arahaki Lagoon and Te Whaiti Nui A Toi Canyon

Rotorua   54
23   Tarawera Falls and Lake Tarawera
24   Lake Okataina Scenic Reserve

Tongariro National Park   56
25   Tongariro Alpine Crossing

Tongariro National Park   58
26   Tama Lakes and Taranaki Falls

Tongariro National Park   60
27   Lake Rotopounamu

Lake Taupo   62
28   Kawakawa Bay

Boundary Stream Scenic Reserve, Hawke's Bay   63
29   Shine Falls

Hawke's Bay   64
30   Otatara Pa Historic Reserve

Hawke's Bay   66
31   Cape Kidnappers Gannet Reserve

Kaweka Forest Park   68
32   Kaweka J
33   Kaweka Flats

Ruahine Forest Park   70
34   Sunrise Hut

Tararua Forest Park   72
35   Mt Holdsworth
36   Atiwhakatu Valley

Wairarapa   74
37   Castlepoint Scenic Reserve

Wairarapa   76
38   Putangirua Pinnacles Scenic Reserve

Egmont National Park   77
39   Dawson Falls and Wilkies Pools
40   Mangorei Track and Pouakai Range

Taranaki   81
41   Whitecliffs Walkway

Whanganui National Park   83
42   Bridge to Nowhere

Wanganui   84
43   Bushy Park

Wellington   86
44   Butterfly Creek, East Harbour Regional Park
45   Orongorongo Track, Rimutaka Forest Park

Tararua Forest Park, Wellington   90
46   Smith Creek and Tawharenikau River

Wellington 92
47 Kapiti Island Nature Reserve

Porirua, Wellington 94
48 Colonial Knob Walkway

Wellington 96
49 Makara Walkway

Puponga Farm Park, Golden Bay 98
50 Wharariki Beach

Abel Tasman National Park 100
51 Totaranui to Separation Point
52 Taupo Point

Abel Tasman National Park 104
53 Te Pukatea Bay and Pitt Head

Kahurangi National Park 106
54 Lake Sylvester and the Lockett Range
55 Asbestos Cottage
56 Mt Arthur and the Tableland
57 Lodestone

Nelson Lakes National Park 110
58 Bushline Hut and Mt Robert
59 Lake Rotoiti

Marlborough Sounds 112
60 Mt Stokes
61 Ship Cove, Queen Charlotte Track

Kaikoura 114
62 Kaikoura Peninsula Walkway

Isolated Hill Scenic Reserve 116
63 Sawcut Gorge

Kahurangi National Park, West Coast 117
64 Heaphy Coastline
65 Oparara Basin

Paparoa National Park, West Coast 120
66 Pororari–Punakaiki Loop

Westport 122
67 Charming Creek Walkway
68 Denniston Walkway

Victoria Forest Park 126
69 Murray Creek Goldfields Track

Westland/Tai Poutini National Park, West Coast 128
70 Alex Knob
71 Harihari Coastal Walk

Westland/Tai Poutini National Park, West Coast 132
72 Okarito Pack Track

Westland/Tai Poutini National Park 134
73 Lake Matheson

Lewis Pass National Reserve 135
74 Lake Daniells

Lewis Pass National Reserve, Canterbury 136
75 Nina Hut
76 Cannibal Gorge
77 Lewis Pass Tops

Port Hills, Canterbury 140
78 Sign of the Packhorse

Arthur's Pass National Park 142
79 Avalanche Peak
80 Otira Valley
81 Bealey Spur and Hut

Canterbury 146
82 Mt Somers

Aoraki/Mount Cook National Park 148
83 Sealy Tarns
84 Hooker Valley

Kanuka Scenic Reserve, Central Otago 150
85 Kanuka Track

West Matukituki Valley, Mount Aspiring National Park 152
86 Aspiring Hut
87 Rob Roy Glacier

The Stack Conservation Area, Wanaka 154
88 Roys Peak

Queenstown 156
89 Ben Lomond Track

Mount Aspiring National Park 158
90 Routeburn Falls, Routeburn Track

Otago Peninsula, Otago 160
91 Sandfly Bay

Fiordland National Park 162
92 Milford Sound Foreshore and Bowen Falls

Fiordland National Park 164
93 Gertrude Saddle

Fiordland National Park 166
94 Key Summit, Routeburn Track
95 Lake Marian

Fiordland National Park 170
96 Shallow Bay

The Catlins, South Otago 172
97 Nugget Point, Cannibal Bay, Purakaunui Falls
98 Catlins River Walk, Catlins Forest Park

Rakiura National Park, Stewart Island 176
99 Maori Beach, Port William
100 Ulva Island, Paterson Inlet

References and further reading

INTRODUCTION

Walking is one of life's great pleasures. Walkers can stride out knowing they are doing something physically good for themselves and probably something good for their minds as well. There is nothing like a good stroll to shake off petty worries, to gain a clean and clear perspective on the burdens of busy, modern lives.

The luxury of spending a decent length of time with your companions is another great aspect of walking. You can walk and talk, but equally, you can walk but feel no compulsion to communicate – companionable silence is acceptable. Equally, walking alone offers great rewards; in your own company you have the luxury of striding at your own pace with your own thoughts.

Not surprisingly, the best walking in New Zealand lies in those parts of the country where nature still holds sway; where streams tumble through forest, where mountains shoulder into the sky and birds chime. It is largely from these areas that the walks in this book are drawn, although there are some in rural and urban settings too.

Walking for pleasure is a pastime with a comparatively short history in New Zealand.

Certainly for Maori and early European explorers, walking provided the main means of getting about. Then, in frequently mountainous and heavily forested terrain, often untracked, walking was usually anything but enjoyable.

Some four decades *after* English poet William Wordsworth was gambolling about the walking tracks of Britain and Europe's scenic spots, and writing romantic verse about the experience, New Zealand explorer Thomas Brunner was struggling through the wilds of the Buller River. In an account of the epic five months he toiled in the Buller, Brunner wrote:

Large granite rocks heaped confusedly together all over the surface, with a thick growth of underbrush and briers, an immense quantity of dead and rotten timber, and all these on the steep and broken declivities of a range of high mountains, interspersed with per-

pendicular walls of rocks, precipices, and deep ravines, form a combination of difficulties which must be encountered to be adequately understood…

Ironically, it was only as the 'wilderness' was tamed, burnt and beaten back that New Zealanders began to truly appreciate walking and scenery for its own sake. With the development of road and rail in New Zealand in the latter half of the nineteenth century, the accessibility of many scenic places increased. The first national park, Tongariro, was formed in 1887, and the first scenic reserves in 1903. Later, in 1954, came the first forest park, Tararua Forest Park.

Early walking tracks followed the routes of Maori trails, gold prospectors and surveyors, but by the early twentieth century tracks were being developed specifically for the pleasure they provided.

A. H. Reed, one of New Zealand's most prodigious walkers (and founder of the country's oldest publishing firm) summed up the pleasure of walking with these words written in 1917:

Life has been aptly likened to a walk. We start out with vim and vigour in the early morning, and, sooner or later, settle down to a steady walk, while at eventide we turn our eyes towards our resting place, from which we look to set out with renewed vigour on the morrow. Sometimes the skies are sunny and sometimes overcast. Now the road [track] is rough and stony, and presently a stretch of grassy sward. Sometimes a stream is crossed, from the cool clear water of which a refreshing draught is taken; or, for awhile we rest under a grove of shady trees… And always there is the mystery and hopeful anticipation of the unknown that lies ahead.

New Zealand's first tramping club, Wellington's Tararua Tramping Club was formed in 1919, and many others began in the 1920s and 1930s. Clubs played a crucial role in providing transport and developing tracks. Later, both the

Department of Lands & Survey and the New Zealand Forest Service actively developed tracks for recreation, until in 1987 both merged to form the Department of Conservation who manage the majority of walks described in this book.

Today, New Zealand rates as one of the best countries in the world for walking. Very few other countries offer such a diversity of terrain, ranging from coastal to mountain, in such a small area. New Zealand has tracks in areas that feature active volcanoes, hot springs, moss-laden rainforests, ragged fault ranges, glacier-carved valleys, island-studded lakes and golden-sand coastlines.

Because New Zealand has been isolated from other landmasses for over 65 million years, much of the flora and fauna here is also unique. Amongst many other examples, creatures like the kea (the only alpine parrot in the world) and plants like the kauri (a tree of great girth and grandeur)

help make the experience of walking here distinctive.

In addition, there are no snakes or savage animals in New Zealand, and the only poisonous spider is the shy and increasingly endangered katipo, the bite of which is almost never fatal.

A Brief Guide to New Zealand's Natural Areas
Fully a third of New Zealand's land area is managed by the Department of Conservation, and by far the majority of walks in this book lie on this land. DOC administers this land under a range of categories that include:

Above The beech forested flanks of the St Arnaud Range, Nelson Lakes National Park

National Parks

New Zealand has 14 national parks ranging from Te Ure-wera National Park in the North Island to Rakiura National Park on Stewart Island. Generally, national parks are large, mountainous and scenically spectacular. The former Department of Lands & Survey had responsibility for managing them (along with scenic reserves) until DOC took over this role in 1987.

Forest Parks

New Zealand has 19 forest parks, ranging from Northland Forest Park to Catlins Forest Park in Otago–Southland. Like national parks, they are generally large and often mountainous, although often have a more subtle beauty. All forest parks were established by the former New Zealand Forest Service between the years 1954 and 1984, partly to complement the country's then growing number of national parks. Today, like national parks, they are managed by DOC.

Scenic Reserves

New Zealand boasts literally hundreds of scenic reserves, ranging from tiny patches of bush to quite large forests. They are the main type of reserve; others include nature reserves (such as Kapiti Island), scientific reserves (such as Tiritiri Matangi Island), recreation reserves, and a national reserve (of which there is only one, at Lewis Pass).

Other Areas

DOC also manages some farm parks, of which the Cape Colville Farm Park (Coromandel Walkway) is just one. In addition to areas managed by DOC, some of the walks covered in this book are maintained by local bodies. In Wellington, for example, the Wellington Regional Council manages a system of regional parks providing many excellent walking opportunities. Similarly, in Auckland, there are several regional parks such as the Waitakere Ranges and Hunua Ranges.

Walkways

Walkways have special status, for they cross land of varying tenure, sometimes including private farmland. Originally the idea, sparked by the Federated Mountain Clubs and Auckland tramper Bob Usheer in the early 1970s, was for a walking track spanning the length of the country. However, the idea was whittled down to a more manageable task, and currently there are 125 walkways. These range from just one kilometre to the 65 kilometre long St James Walkway.

Taking dogs

Dogs are prohibited on all tracks in national parks, wildlife refuges and nature reserves. For other areas, such as forest and regional parks, dogs are often permitted unless they pose a risk to local populations of ground birds such as kiwi or weka. Where the tracks pass through sections of farmland, as do many walkways, local farmers may not allow dogs which could disrupt stock. If dogs are prohibited this is usually indicated on the sign at the start of the walk.

Walk selection

Walks selected for this book were chosen from throughout New Zealand, reflecting a range of length, difficulty, terrain and natural history. They were selected to suit a range of abilities from the novice walker to the experienced. Very few of the walks featured are beyond the abilities of a moderately fit person with some tramping experience. None involve any serious off-track travel, and generally tracks are well marked and of a high standard.

Selecting what I consider to be the best of the country's walks was necessarily subjective. I have tried to cover a range of scenery, length and difficulty, while at the same time making the coverage nationwide. Although someone else might argue for an entirely different list, together the 100 walks detailed here reflect the great diversity of New Zealand walking.

Length and difficulty

Each walk is classified according to difficulty, which readers should note depends very much on conditions. Wet weather could very well turn a medium tramp into a hard, or even impossible one, while winter snow may transform a medium trip into one that requires mountaineering skills. When selecting a walk it is important to take the abilities of all party members into consideration.

Each walk is classified 'easy', 'medium' or 'hard' with some in between. By far the majority fall into the 'easy' or 'medium' categories.

Easy: Expect gentle terrain, well-marked tracks, no river crossings, and walking times of 2–3 hours.

Medium: The walker may come across un-bridged river crossings, steep sections of track, or some travel on open tops. Travel times could be 5–6 hours per day.

Hard: These trips will often entail walking for more than 6 hours, may involve steeper sections of terrain where a head for heights is preferable and navigation skills required.

A note on walking times

Walkers must expect some variation in times depending on conditions. In summer a hard-baked track will provide much firmer and faster footing than the same track churned to mud in winter. I have tried to tailor times for the likely ability of walkers in each grade. For example, a fit and experienced walker will probably be able to halve some of the times suggested for an 'easy' walk. Conversely, an inexperienced and less fit walker will struggle to match the times suggested by a 'hard' walk. In other words, the easier the walk, the more generous the time given.

Alternative routes

Wherever possible, both shorter and longer alternatives to the walk described are mentioned. Some walks that pass huts offer the possibility of turning the walk into an over-night tramp. For this reason, details of hut capacity have been included.

Keeping information up to date

Although every effort has been made to ensure information in this guide is both correct and up to date, please remember that wild places change constantly. Floods alter rivers,

Above Lake Okataina, Rotorua, at sunset

volcanoes erupt from time to time and storms or earthquakes can devastate forests and tracks. Furthermore, the condition of tracks varies according to how recently they have been maintained. For these reasons, trampers should always check with the local Department of Conservation (DOC) visitor centre for updates before their intended trip. The relevant DOC telephone number has been given for each tramp. DOC's website www.doc.govt.nz is also an excellent source of information.

If you do find any safety hazards – such as a bridge washed out, or a new slip on a track – please report it. Tel: DOC HOTline, or Tel: 0800 362 468.

Maps

The maps in this book are digital images created by Roger Smith, the director of Geographx, a Wellington-based company that specialises in advanced digital mapping. Roger's superb maps – perhaps oblique panoramas are a better description – do what no photograph can achieve: offer a complete overview of each tramp, showing tracks, huts, and major features. For more information, refer to *Landforms: the shaping of New Zealand*, in Further Reading.

While these maps indicate tracks, huts and major topographical features, they are not intended to be used for navigation. No map will be necessary for many of the easy and some of the medium walks, but if in doubt you should purchase a NZMS 260 series 1:50,000 scale topographical map or appropriate track map. The correct map(s) number for each tramp is included in the fact file at the end of each chapter. Note that 'true left' refers to the left bank of a river when facing downstream, and 'true right' to the right bank. For some of the regional parks in the Auckland region, the brochures produced by the Auckland Regional Council are often more accurate and useful than the topographical maps.

Seasons and weather

New Zealand's temperate latitude fools some visitors to this country into thinking that the weather will always be mild. Although tempered by its maritime surrounds, New Zealand's position in the path of the 'Roaring 40s' and its mountainous terrain combine to produce some of the most changeable and unpredictable climate on the planet.

In the mountains, where many of the walks in this book are located, snow can fall at any time of year, although obviously is rarer during summer. Some parts of New Zealand, particularly the West Coast and Fiordland, experience some of the highest rainfall in the world – some 7–9 metres of rain falls at Milford Sound annually, while one year a West Coast valley near Hokitika received over 15 metres of rain. Heavy rain can, on rare occasions, make sections of some tracks or stream crossings impassable.

Walkers need to respect and plan around the weather. Always obtain a forecast before you leave, and be prepared to pare back or change your plans accordingly.

As a general rule, late summer and autumn (January to April) are the best months for walking in the South Island. During these times the temperatures are at their mildest, the rainfall is generally less, and the probability of snow unlikely. Spring and early summer (September to December) offers the delights of alpine flowers, but in very mountainous terrain avalanches may pose a risk. For those who are suitably equipped and experienced, winter (May to August) offer its own rewards: generally fewer people, sometimes crisp, long spells of fine weather, and all the glories of snow-capped mountains. In the North Island, excepting the central plateau, Mt Taranaki and main axis mountain ranges, walkers can expect milder, snow-free weather all year round. For further information check out: www.metservice.co.nz and www.avalanche.net.nz

Water, rubbish and conservation

The quality of water available on any particular track depends on its location. For rural and coastal walks, it is advisable to carry your own water. However, in more mountainous back-country areas, you can most likely still safely drink straight from streams. The water-borne parasite Giardia is present in some streams and lakes, so if in doubt, carry water treatments or use a water filter.

Take care when toileting. If there is no longdrop, go to the toilet at least 100 metres away from water sources, and bury your wastes in a shallow 'cat scrape.'

Have consideration for the environment; don't take anything natural, and don't leave anything unnatural. Carry out all your rubbish and any you find.

Safety and equipment

There is not the scope in this book to give a detailed description of equipment and safety, but a brief list of what should be carried for a typical medium or hard day walk is as follows: warm woolly hat, sunhat, gloves, raincoat, warm jersey or fleece, pair of polypropylene or woollen longjohns, wool or polypropylene top, a pair of shorts, first-aid kit, map, compass, sunscreen, and enough food for the trip duration plus a few extra emergency snacks. Obviously many of these items will be superfluous on a short, coastal walk in summer.

For hard trips you may want to take a flysheet and sleeping mat in case of an emergency night out. In winter you may need to add ice axe, crampons, sunglasses, more warm gear, and extra food. Check out the New Zealand Mountain Safety Council's *Bushcraft Manual* for more information. The Mountain Safety Council also has many good brochures and manuals on safety in the outdoors www.mountainsafety.org.nz

Intentions

Signing an intentions book at the track start does not guarantee that anyone will notice you have become overdue. Walkers must leave their intentions, including possible bad weather alternatives, with a trusted friend who can, in the event of your party becoming overdue, be relied upon to contact the police Search and Rescue (SAR): Tel 111 and ask for police. If you pass by huts during your walk, sign the hut book so that your route can be followed in the event you become overdue or have an accident.

Finally, happy walking!

Above *Stone hut ruins and cart, Logantown, Otago Goldfields Park*

NORTHLAND
CAPE REINGA COASTAL WALKWAY

Contrary to popular opinion, Cape Reinga is not the northern-most tip of New Zealand's mainland; that title belongs to the Surville Cliffs of North Cape, which lie a full 2 kilometres closer to the equator.

Despite this geographic shortcoming, Cape Reinga is a place of surreal beauty. Between five and two million years ago, the area consisted of islands, but in the last million years

huge quantities of sand, deposited by oceanic currents, created a connection with the mainland. Now, only the islands around Cape Maria van Diemen remain separated.

Cape Reinga is also of immense importance to Maori, who know it as Te Rerenga Wairua. Here, according to legend, the spirits of the deceased at last depart Aotearoa to begin the long journey back to the ancestral homeland of Hawaiiki-A-Nui.

While most of the 200,000 people who visit the cape are content to wander the short sealed path to the lighthouse and gaze over the often-turbulent waters at the meeting of the Tasman Sea and Pacific Ocean, walkers will find a rewarding walkway loop track to Cape Maria van Diemen and Twilight Beach. The walkway crosses some of New Zealand's most distinctive coastal scenery.

Cape Reinga to Cape Maria van Diemen turnoff 2–2.5 hours

Branching off the path to the lighthouse, a well-benched track descends for 30 minutes beside coastal cliffs, down to the long sweep of Te Werahi Beach. After following the coast southwards for 45–60 minutes, the track crosses Te Werahi Stream (sometimes impassable after mid-tide) before heading inland up grassy slopes to colourful dunes beyond, dominated by the native sand plants pingao and spinifex. A gentle climb leads over the flanks of Herangi Hill (159 m) to a signposted track junction which offers fine views of Cape Maria van Diemen and its offshore islands. On a good day the side track leading to the cape proves rewarding (90 minutes return).

Cape Maria van Diemen turnoff to Twilight Beach and Cape Reinga Road 3–4 hours

From the track junction, the main walkway enters coastal shrublands, dominated by prostrate manuka, traversing a broad ledge above the cliffs of Maungatiketike and Pitokuku points before descending through lupins towards Twilight Beach. From a signposted track junction, the 5 minute walk to Twilight Beach is worthwhile. Back at the junction head

inland through a vast area of dunes, with some curiously charred and eroding rock exposed in places. Here large orange squares atop tall poles indicate the route at intervals. A short section of dense lupins leads to a sidle through twisted manuka forest and out into the open again beside an extensive wetland in the Te Werahi Valley. The track crosses a narrow neck of the raupo-dominated wetland on a boardwalk to a final manuka stand before reaching farmland. Across a stile, poles lead up grassy slopes to a farm ridge, which is followed to Te Werahi Gate on the Cape Reinga Road. Most walkers will choose to walk – or hitchhike – the 4.5 kilometres of road back to the cape (the shortest option), but there is the choice of using a track that reconnects with the walkway back at Te Werahi Beach.

Opposite *Sand dunes and rock with Cape Maria van Diemen beyond*

Grade Medium–Hard
Map M02 North Cape
Total Walking Time 6–7 hours return (including 90 minute side trip to Cape Maria van Diemen)
Access From Kaitaia take SH 1 north as far as it goes. Allow 90 minutes to drive the 112 km from Kaitaia, which is sealed except for the last 20 km. The cape has a carpark, toilets and information panels. Plans to develop a visitor centre and seal the remaining section of road are afoot.
Alternative route For those who don't want to complete the entire circuit described above, an equally rewarding option is the trip from Cape Reinga to Cape Maria van Diemen and return. East of Cape Reinga a pleasant walk leads to Tapotupotu Bay and a carpark and campsite there (allow 90 minutes each way).
Information DOC Kaitaia Tel: 09-408-6014

BREAM HEAD SCENIC RESERVE, WHANGAREI
TE WHARA TRACK

At the head of Whangarei Harbour several peaks rise mono-lithically, their sheerness and close proximity to the sea lending them a stature that belies their modest heights. At 475 metres Bream Head–Te Whara is the highest of these, the eroded stump of a volcano that formed 20 million years ago; Manaia and Mt Lion are the other two prominent peaks.

Botanically, Bream Head is of national importance, con-taining Northland's largest remaining broadleaf–pohutukawa forest and some locally endemic species. Like many other areas in New Zealand, Bream Head has attracted the attention of lo-cal conservationists who plan to develop a pest-free haven for such species as kaka, which they hope will begin to breed in the reserve.

Of the many walks available in the area, the Te Whara Track is the most challenging, and follows the route of an his-toric Ngatiwai trail. It links Ocean Beach with Urquharts Bay, traversing en route the summits of Bream Head and Mt Lion, with a side trip to Peach Cove possible too. Walkers can expect some steep and slippery terrain, on a well-marked but un-formed tramping track. However, the rewards are outstanding views, superb sandy beaches and much of historic interest too. Carry plenty of drinking water.

Ocean Beach to Bream Head and Peach Cove Track Junction 2.5–3 hours

Follow the white sands of Ocean Beach southwards for 5 minutes before picking up a track that climbs up onto grassy slopes. Views of the Bream Islands and the more distant Poor Knights Islands soon unfold. After about 40 minutes climbing, past a small lighthouse, the track reaches an old World War II naval radar station base built in 1942. Although little remains of the station buildings, the rusting radar is visible, tucked into the nearby bush with the dramatic rock spire known as the Old Woman beyond.

The track enters forest and continues to climb until reaching the ridge crest near Bream Head. A side track leads up to a viewpoint on the head (475 m), but it will tempt only the more agile walkers who have a good head for heights. On a good day walkers can see as far south as Cape Rodney and as far north as Cape Brett.

Further along the ridge is another large rock outcrop known appropriately as the Black Thumb, which is some-times tackled by rock climbers. A descent through the lush forest leads down to open forest with a grassy clearing, where a track branches off to Ocean Beach Road. About 10 minutes further on is the Peach Cove Track junction.

Side Track to Peach Cove Hut (8 bunks, $10/night, locked) 40–60 minutes return

A steep descent through coastal forest leads down slopes to Peach Cove, a small sandy bay set in a bouldery coastline and overhung by pohutukawa. Peach Cove Hut, renovated by DOC in 2002, is set back in the bush, near an astonishing pohutukawa growing atop a gigantic boulder. To stay in the hut, which is locked, you must book through DOC.

Manaia, Bream Head and Mt Lion at dusk from the Whangarei Heads Road

Peach Cove Track to Urquharts Bay 2.5–3 hours

Back on the ridge, the main Te Whara track begins an undulating climb towards Mt Lion, passing more rock pinnacles en route. The vegetation restricts the views from Mt Lion (395 m). Beyond, the track begins a steepish descent towards Urquharts Bay, with a good glimpse of Smugglers Bay through the trees at one point. The track intercepts the Smugglers Bay Track just past where it opens out onto farmland. Head right for 10 minutes to reach Urquharts Bay.

Grade Medium–Hard
Total Walking Time 5–6 hours through trip; add 40–60 minutes for side trip to Peach Cove
Map Q07 Whangarei
Access From Whangarei take Riverside Drive, Whangarei Heads Road and Ocean Beach Road to reach a DOC carpark at Ocean Beach, which has toilets and an information panel. Allow about 40 minutes to drive the 30 km from Whangarei. The Te Whara Track ends at Urquharts Bay, 5 km away from Ocean Beach by road.

Alternative route Several excellent shorter walks are possible: Peach Cove Track (2 hours return from Ocean Beach Road), Busby Head and Smugglers Bay Track (1–1.5 hour round trip), Peach Cove–Bream Head–Ocean Beach loop (3–3.5 hours).
Information DOC Whangarei Tel: 09-430-2133, Bream Head Conservation Trust: www.breamheadtrust.org.nz

PUKETI FOREST, NORTHLAND FOREST PARK
WAIHOANGA GORGE KAURI WALK

Northland Forest Park, gazetted in 1984, was the last of the forest parks established by the New Zealand Forest Service before its demise in 1987. The park encompasses several discrete but significant areas of forest, largely dominated by kauri, of which the best known is Waipoua Forest – home of New Zealand's largest remaining kauri tree, Tane Mahuta.

Puketi Forest does not boast any giants to equal Tane Mahuta, but it does offer a better range of walks. Perhaps the best is the Waihoanga Gorge Kauri Walk, an easy loop track through a dense area of kauri that will suit walkers of most abilities and will also appeal to children.

Walkers may like to stay at nearby Puketi Forest Hut, a comfortable 24-bunk hut with a fridge, stove, and hot shower, which can be booked through DOC and makes an excellent base from which to explore the area.

Puketi Road to Waihoanga Gorge Kauri Walk and return 1.5–2 hours
Cross a stile over a fence and follow marker poles over farmland for 5 minutes to another stile (walkers may have to negotiate electric fences). Here the track descends across another paddock to the bush boundary, with a good view of the heavily-forested ridges of Puketi Forest. Even from this distance the kauri dominate, their large crowns bristling through the canopy. Immediately after entering the forest the track crosses a wooden footbridge over the Waihoanga River, which spills into a gorge downstream. The well-formed, graded track wends through lush and dense forest, with some sections of boardwalk. A platform offers a disappointing view downstream, while a better one looks back at a waterfall in the Waihoanga River.

After curling around a substantial kauri, the first encountered, the track climbs gently up a ridge to the fork of a loop track. The loop is of tramping track standard, but is no longer benched, and can be muddy and rooty in places.

Take the right-hand branch through an avenue of tall kauri to reach the highest point of the loop at a signposted junction (here a tramping track branches off to Pukatea Ridge). The other half of the loop descends towards the Waihoanga River again, threading through more sizeable kauri, which impress more with their height than their stoutness. A brief climb ensues to complete the loop back on the main track.

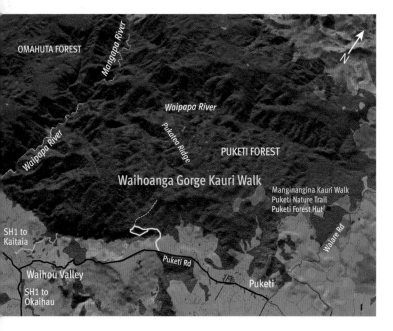

Grade Easy
Total Walking Time 1.5–2 hours return
Map P05 Kaikohe
Access From SH 1, 8 km from the township of Okaihau, turn off onto Puketi Road and follow this for 9 km. The Waihoanga Gorge Kauri Walk is well signposted.
Alternative route Several other walks are available in Puketi Forest. Manginangina Kauri Walk (15 minutes, suitable for wheelchairs), the Puketi Nature Trail (1 hour), the Omahuta Kauri Sanctuary Walk (30 minutes) and the Pukekohe Stream Track (3 hours).
Information DOC Russell Tel: 09-403-9005, Email: russellvc@doc.govt.nz

WHANGAMUMU SCENIC RESERVE
WHANGAMUMU HARBOUR, BAY OF ISLANDS

Whangamumu Harbour is a sheltered inlet near the base of the peninsula that stretches out to end at Cape Brett. Maori once occupied the attractive natural harbour, and between 1890 and 1940 European whalers made a base here too. At Net Rock, north of the harbour, humpback whales were caught with large nets fixed by a wire cable across a narrow channel – apparently the only place in the world where this fishing technique was employed. Using longboats, the whalers drove the humpbacks into the nets, where the entangled whales were sufficiently slowed to be easily harpooned, then dragged back to the whaling base for boiling down. In its peak year, 1927, the station produced some 388 tons of oil from 74 whales. The station finally closed after an oil slick from a wrecked ship forced the whales to alter their migration path.

From a lay-by on Rawhiti Road, the walk crosses farmland, then climbs a forested ridge to descend to Whangamumu Harbour. It will suit walkers of modest abilities and families with school-age children. Carry water.

Rawhiti Road to Whangamumu Harbour
1–1.5 hours

Cross a stile over a fence and take the track over boggy farmland for 10–15 minutes before entering the forest, dominated by manuka and tree ferns. The first part of the track is gravelled, but the latter part comprises open clay, which can be slippery after rain. After a fairly easy 140 metre climb, the track reaches the ridge crest, where a trail branches off (it joins the Cape Brett Track after passing through a kauri grove). The track to Whangamumu leads down through forest before emerging onto grassy slopes with good views of the harbour. Puriri and pohutukawa shade the idyllic sandy shore. Head left at the beach, past a DOC information panel, and around a cove to where a track climbs briefly around a headland to reach the old whaling station. Concrete building foundations, rusting boilers and an old slipway still remain, as does a stone dome with historic photographs and information on the station's history. Even given such evidence of the past, it is difficult to imagine 20 people living here over the winter whaling season.

Grade Easy
Total Walking Time 2.5–3 hours return
Map Q05 Bay of Islands
Access From Russell drive for 27 km on Russell, Kempthorne and Manawaora roads before turning left onto Rawhiti Road. The track start is signposted on the right, 1 km along Rawhiti Road. Secure parking is available on private land nearby for a small fee.
Alternative route From Whangamumu Bay, fit and experienced walkers could complete a loop using tracks to Te Toroa Bay, the Cape Brett Track, and back via the Kauri Grove track. Allow 4.5–5 hours for this round trip.
Information DOC Russell Tel: 09-403-9005
Email: russellvc@doc.govt.nz

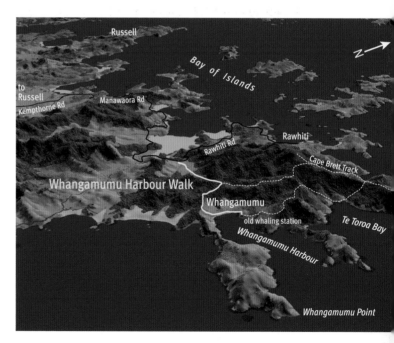

WAITAKERE RANGES REGIONAL PARK
KAREKARE–PARARAHA • MONTANA HERITAGE TRAIL

KAREKARE–PARARAHA

Ironsand beaches, windswept headlands and luxuriant coastal forests all combine to make the Waitakere coastline a favourite haunt of Aucklanders. Whilst Waitakere mayor, Bob Harvey described it as 'the untamed coast' in his first book, and dedicated an entire second book, Rolling Thunder, *to one of those beaches, Karekare, where this walk begins and ends.*

From Karekare the route takes the Zion Hill and Buck Taylor tracks to Pararaha, a place of freshwater wetlands, large dunes and black volcanic cliffs. From here the walk swings northwards, headed along the shore, through an old railway tunnel, around some cliffs where the Tasman Sea pounds in, and past the protruding thumb of Paratahi Island back to Karekare. It will appeal to walkers of moderate fitness.

Karekare to Pararaha Stream 1.5–2 hours

From the carpark take the Pohutukawa Glade Walk to a picnic area, where the Zion Hill Track starts. It climbs steadily up a forested spur, with some good views back over Karekare beach and The Watchman. Pohutukawa, puriri, manuka and kawakawa dominate the forest. After 20–25 minutes the track crests Zion Hill (272 m) where the Zion Ridge Track branches off. Continue on the Zion Hill Track through nikau palms, rimu, tree ferns and occasional kauri along an undulating ridge, which can be muddy and slippery. Beyond a small stream a kauri grove boasts some sizeable trees. Cross a second stream to join the Buck Taylor Track, and head right down to a coastal wetland in the Pararaha valley.

Pararaha Stream to Karekare 1.5–2 hours

Pass a track branching upstream (to the Pararaha campsite), and continue downstream towards the coast; note the Pararaha Stream can be impassable after heavy rain.

An unmarked trail leads through large sand dunes and swings northwards towards Karekare. Pass a campsite at Tunnel Point, where an old railway engine (a remnant from kauri milling days) is shaded by pohutukawa, and walk through the tunnel to the beach beyond. Here the blunt cliffs of Cowan Point meet the Tasman Sea. Rock platforms

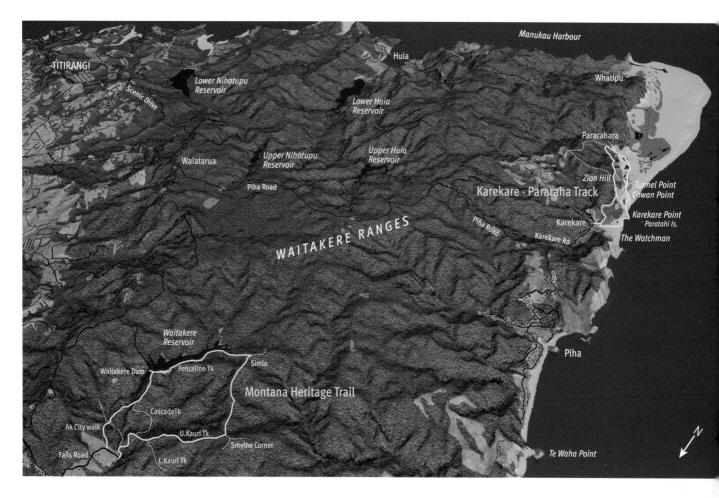

Map labels:
Manukau Harbour
TITIRANGI
Huia
Whatipu
Lower Nihotupu Reservoir
Scenic Drive
Lower Huia Reservoir
Pararahara
Walatarua
Upper Nihotupu Reservoir
Upper Huia Reservoir
Zion Hill
Piha Road
Tunnel Point
Cowan Point
Karekare - Pararaha Track
WAITAKERE RANGES
Piha Road
Karekare Point
Paratahi Is.
Karekare
Karekare Rd
The Watchman
Waitakere Reservoir
Piha
Waitakere Dam
Fenceline Tk
Simla
Montana Heritage Trail
CascadeTk
Ak City walk
U.Kauri Tk
Smythe Corner
L.Kauri Tk
Falls Road
Te Waha Point

just before Karekare Point that used to be dangerous at high tide are now sand-covered and the route is accessible in all but stormy spring tides. Beyond Karekare Point, The Watchman hoves into view again, leading to a short stroll inland to the carpark.

Opposite The distinctive form of nikau palms, Zion Hill Track

Grade Easy–Medium
Maps Q11 Waitakere, Terralink Hunua and Waitakere map
Total Walking Time 3–4 hours.
Access From the Auckland suburb of Titirangi, follow Scenic Drive for 10 km then turn left onto Piha Road. Follow this for 11 km, and turn left onto Karekare Road. A further 3 km takes you down to the road end where there is a carpark, picnic area and toilets.
Alternative route Walkers wanting a shorter stroll may prefer the walk down the coast from Karekare to Tunnel Point (2 hours return).
Information Auckland Regional Council, Arataki Visitor Centre Tel: 09 817 0077. www.arc.govt.nz

MONTANA HERITAGE TRAIL

Aucklanders are blessed with 22 excellent regional parks, all managed by the Auckland Regional Council. Perhaps the best known is the Waitakere Ranges Regional Park, which boasts some 250 kilometres of tracks in the densely forested hills west of Auckland.

This recently developed, high-quality loop walk combines several tracks in the Cascade–Kauri area to make one of the best round trips in the ranges. Montana Wines helped finance an upgrade of existing trails in partnership with the regional council. Some of Auckland's largest remaining kauri – saved from loggers by the Auckland City Council in 1925 – form the highlight. The trail will appeal to walkers and family groups of moderate fitness. As there are a potentially confusing number of trails in the area, ensure you follow the trail indicated by the Montana badge at each junction.

Cascade Track and Upper Kauri Track to Long Road Track 1.5–2 hours

From the Falls Road carpark, cross a footbridge over the Waitakere River and follow the trail up the true left bank for 5 minutes to a junction. Here a large carved Maori statue, or pou, acts as a symbolic guardian for the forest.

Turn right onto the recently upgraded Upper Kauri Track, which zigzags uphill on a mixture of boardwalks and steps through an attractive avenue of adolescent kauri. The Cascade Track branches off near a knoll dominated by size-able kauri. Past the Lower Kauri Track turnoff, undulating ridge travel leads to a track junction near Smythe Corner through forest now decidedly second-hand. Smythe Corner commemorates a family who farmed the area.

Fenceline and Cascade tracks and Auckland City Walk to Falls Road 2–2.5 hours

Head left (southwards) along the Long Road Track, which is being upgraded to a gravelled path. Some 45 minutes along this section the Fenceline Track branches off. This newly routed track sidles above the Waitakere Reservoir, with a viewpoint over the lake en route. Depending on water levels this can be an attractive body of water or an eyesore of exposed earth. Where the Fenceline Track reaches the Saddle Dam, take a worthwhile diversion along to the main Waitakere Dam. This offers good views into the Cascade Kauri Park, fair bristling with towering kauri.

After departing Saddle Dam continue along Fenceline Track as it undulates towards the junction with Cascade Track, passing en route an impressive kauri with a diameter of some 2 metres or so. At the junction with Cascade Track take the right hand fork and follow Cascade Track down the steps to the Auckland City Walk. Another large kauri dominates the track junction here. Turn right, and cross a footbridge over the Waitakere River (here a thin trickle). The well-benched track passes a 1000 year old kauri, and climbs gently to reach the Falls Road picnic area next to the carpark.

Grade Medium

Total Walking Time 3–4 hours return

Maps Q11 Waitakere, Terralink Hunua and Waitakere map

Access Falls Road is about 30 minutes drive from Auckland city. From Swanson take Scenic Drive and Te Henga Road before turning off onto Falls Road. At Falls Road there are toilets, a picnic area and information panels. Note that gates controlling access to the area are locked outside daylight hours. The Arataki Visitor Centre, 20 km from the start of the track on Scenic Drive, is well worth a visit.

Alternative route The Cascade Track or Auckland City Walk form convenient loop tracks for those wanting shorter excursions.

Information Auckland Regional Council, Arataki Visitor Centre Tel: 09-817-0077, www.arc.govt.nz

---

Opposite Trunk patterns on a Kauri tree, Fenceline Track, Montana Heritage Trail

HAURAKI GULF
RANGITOTO ISLAND

Of all Auckland's myriad volcanoes, Rangitoto Island is the youngest; a basaltic mound that erupted out of the sea only 600 years ago in a series of events witnessed by local Maori. The island's low slopes, rising to three mounds, form perhaps the most memorable and distinctive landmark in Auckland.

Undoubtedly the most popular walk on the island is the Summit Track, which begins and ends at the Rangitoto Wharf. Suitable for most walkers, this track crosses the harsh scoria environment upon which the island's forest – dominated by pohutukawa – somehow thrives. DOC's efforts in the 1990s saw the eradication of pests such as possums and wallabies, which had until then adversely affected the island's flora.

Access to the island, a scenic reserve managed by DOC, is by ferry, private boat or sea kayak. Take your own water, and plenty of sun protection during summer.

Rangitoto Wharf to Summit on Summit Track
1–1.5 hours

After disembarking at the wharf, follow the road past the shelter and toilets to the signposted track start. The well-benched, broad and gravelled track begins an almost-imperceptible climb, with occasional openings in the forest providing outward views. Information panels explain the area's natural and human history. After 30–40 minutes, the Wilson's Park track branches off (an alternative way to and from the summit). The main track begins a steady upward plod, reaching another track junction after 5 minutes. Here, a side trail to some lava caves is worth a 15 minute return diversion.

Back on the main summit track, continue a steepening but never very strenuous ascent up to the 259-metre summit. An old World War II command post provides some shelter, and viewing platforms offer superb views, both into the crater and outwards. Only here does the island's roughly circular shape unfold, with a superb panorama of the Hauraki Gulf beyond. Auckland city lies west and southwards, while

Lichen-covered scoria, Rangitoto Island

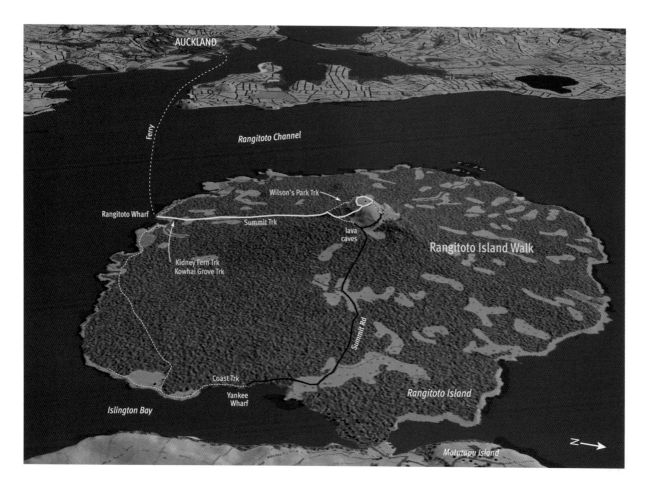

Motutapu Island lies eastwards, connected to Rangitoto by a causeway. Further east Motuihe and Waiheke islands dominate the horizon. A short loop circles the summit's scoria crater. For variety, return via the Wilson's Park track.

Grade Easy

Map R11 Auckland

Access From Auckland take a Fullers Ferry which runs regularly (Tel: 09-367-9102, Email: enquiries@fullers.co.nz). Alternatively, those suitably experienced could hire sea kayaks from Orakei to make the crossing. Toilets and a shelter are available near the wharf. Although no camping is permitted on Rangitoto, neighbouring Motutapu Island has a DOC campground.

Alternative route The Kidney Fern and Kowhai Grove are accessible on a short 30–40 minute loop track from Rangitoto Wharf. Another option is the Coast Track, which circles the island's southeastern shores to end at Yankee Wharf (2–3 hours return). The latter track can be linked with the Summit Track by using a section of the Summit Road, allowing a longer round trip of about 4–5 hours.

Information DOC Auckland Tel: 09-307-9279, Email: aucklandconservancy@doc.govt.nz

HAURAKI GULF
TIRITIRI MATANGI ISLAND

Like many of Auckland's islands, Tiritiri Matangi experienced a period of farming which stripped away much of its native flora and fauna. In 1971 stock was removed from the island, but regeneration of native plants proved slow. During the late 1970s, Auckland University professors John Craig and Neil Mitchell proposed the then radical idea of making the island into an open sanctuary, a place the local community could visit and become involved in tree planting, restoration and pest control.

Between 1984 and 1994 volunteers planted over 250,000 trees, and kiore were eradicated in 1993. The island's rapid transformation has exceeded even the most optimistic greenies' hopes: from just 6 per cent cover in 1980, native vegetation now cloaks 60 per cent of the island. Little spotted kiwi, tieke (saddleback), kokako, takahe, hihi (stitchbird) and kakariki are amongst the 11 species of bird that have been reintroduced and now thrive on the island.

Tiritiri has its own resident rangers, a lighthouse and visitor centre, and guides who offer the possibility of a tour. Independent walkers can choose from a number of tracks, all well signposted, ranging from 30 minutes to 5 hours. A 3 hour round trip is described below. Maps of the island, available for purchase, help fund projects on the island.

Access to the island, a scientific reserve managed jointly by DOC and the Supporters of Tiritiri Matangi, is by ferry from either Auckland or Whangaparaoa. Take your own food and water.

Lighthouse, Tiritiri Matangi Island

Tiritiri Wharf , Hobbs Beach, Kawerau Track to Ridge Track 1–1.5 hours

From the wharf head north along the Hobbs Beach Track for 10 minutes. Fringed by large pohutukawa, Hobbs Beach has toilets, good swimming and a picnic area. Here take the Kawerau Track, which climbs using a series of boardwalks and steps through a densely forested gully of mature trees including kohekohe, puriri and pohutukawa. In places there are exquisite line drawings on information panels explaining natural history. The Kawerau Track slopes up to meet the Ridge Track, which runs along the island's backbone.

Ridge Track to lighthouse, return to wharf via Wattle Track 1–1.5 hours

The Ridge Track, essentially a mown path, heads along the island's crest towards the lighthouse at the south of the island. This is an enjoyable stroll, passing many former tree-planting sites en route, and walkers are likely to encounter takahe feeding on the grass. The Ridge Track crests a grassy

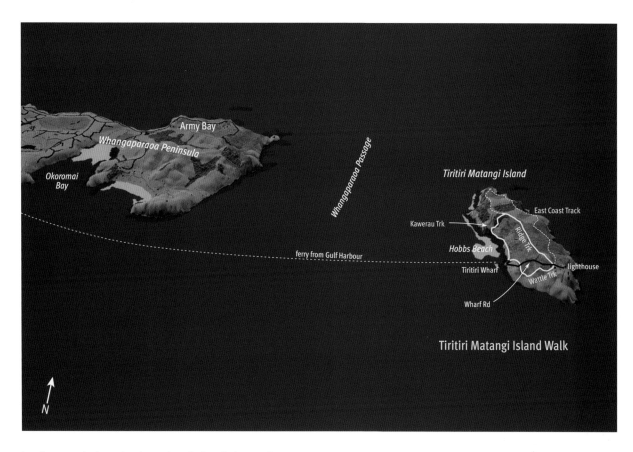

Tiritiri Matangi Island Walk

knoll to reach the Wharf Road and, shortly beyond, a visitor centre where there is complimentary tea and coffee. An adjacent shop sells souvenirs, books and drinks. Toilets are located nearby.

The neighbouring lighthouse (built in 1863) and surrounds offer good views of the island and Hauraki Gulf. Five minutes back down Wharf Road, take the Wattle Track, one of the best places from which to observe tui, tieke, bellbirds, robins and whiteheads. The well-benched, gravelled track wends through bush gullies, with occasional views towards Auckland and Rangitoto Island, to end on the Wharf Road, just 2 minutes from the wharf.

Grade Easy
Map R11 Auckland
Total Walking Time 2–3 hours return
Access 360 Discovery runs trips to Tiritiri Matangi from either Auckland or Gulf Harbour (on the Whangaparaoa Peninsula) allowing about 5 hours on the island (Tel: 0800-888-006, Email: info@360discovery.co.nz). At the Tiritiri Wharf there is a shelter, toilets and information panels.

Alternative route Those wanting a longer 3–4 hour walk can extend the circuit described above by using the East Coast Track instead of the Ridge Track.
Information DOC Auckland Tel: 09-307-9279, Email: aucklandconservancy@doc.govt.nz
Supporters of Tiritiri Matangi Inc. www.tiritirimatangi.org.nz

TAWHARANUI REGIONAL PARK
MAORI BAY COAST WALK

Tawharanui, another regional park managed by the Auckland Regional Council, occupies a peninsula east of Warkworth that juts out into the sea overlooking Kawau Island. It's a place of gnarled pohutukawa, regenerating native forest, rolling farmland and secluded beaches. Established in 1973, the reserve is now an open sanctuary with a predator-proof fence across the peninsula protecting flora and fauna from pests. North Island brown kiwi were reintroduced in November 2006. A marine reserve has also been established off the northern shoreline.

Happily such parks provide places where simple pursuits like walking and enjoying nature have precedence; outposts against the relentless development overtaking many areas of coastal Auckland and Northland. The walk described here encompasses all the elements of the park, with some travel on farmland, some on beaches and some through bush. It suits walkers of moderate fitness and experience; part of the route involves unmarked travel over bouldery beaches.

The highly endangered New Zealand dotterel nests in places on the shore, and walkers are requested to avoid their fenced-off breeding sites.

Lagoon Carpark to Maori Bay 1 hour

From the carpark, the track leads past the lagoon to reach Jones Bay. At Jones Bay, head along the shoreline on the southern side of the peninsula. Travel across a mixture of bouldery beaches, pebbly shores and rocky platforms, past Scow Point, to reach Maori Bay after about an hour. Flat-topped Kawau Island lies offshore.

Maori Bay to Trig via Fishermans and South Coast Tracks 25–30 minutes

From Maori Bay, the steepish Fishermans Track climbs grassy slopes to reach a signposted junction on the South Coast Track. Head right. The track passes through a small stand of manuka before crossing a stile onto farmland. Follow wooden marker posts along farm tracks for 15–20 minutes to reach the trig station on the crest of the peninsula, where there are excellent views of Little Barrier Island and Coromandel Peninsula. A worthwhile side trip is the track (muddy in winter) that leads to an excellent lookout over Tokatu Point (an extra 30–40 minutes return).

Little Barrier Island from North Coast Track, Tawharanui Regional Park

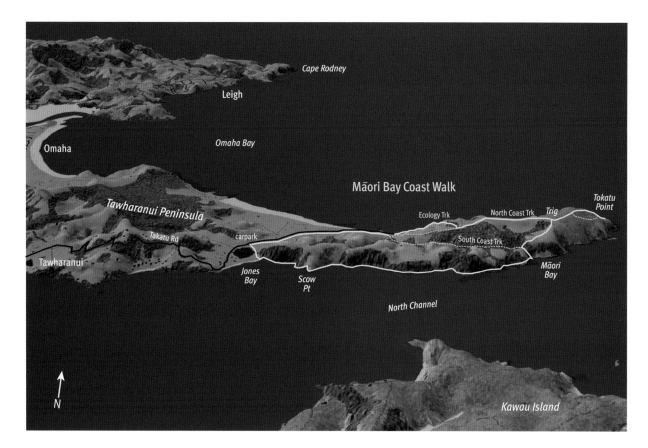

Trig to Lagoon Carpark via North Coast and Ecology Tracks 1.5–2 hours

From the trig follow farm tracks across cattle-grazed paddocks to where a gravel road begins. Follow this for 5 minutes before diverting down the Ecology Track. This wide, benched, grassy track wends into a shallow gully before emerging at the bouldery coastline. Follow a route around the coast to sandy Anchor Bay, and turn inland before Flat Rock to reach the road. An information centre and toilets are located nearby. To reach the carpark, either walk along the road, or – if energy and enthusiasm persist – use a trail that climbs to the South Coast Track and ends at the Lagoon Carpark.

Grade Easy–Medium
Maps R09 Warkworth, Tawharanui Regional Park brochure
Total Walking Time 2.5–3.5 hours
Access At Warkworth, turn off SH 1 onto Matakana Road and drive to Matakana. Takatu Road branches off 1.5 km beyond Matakana and ends at the park after 14 km. The Lagoon Carpark is situated near Jones Bay, where there are toilets, an information panel (with a map) and a picnic area. A locked gate prevents vehicle access to the South Coast Track carpark (at the end of Takatu Road) during the hours of darkness. There's a large camping area at West End sector of Tawharanui; bookings are essential during the busy summer period.
Information Auckland Regional Council Tel: 09-366-2000, Email: info@arc.govt.nz, Tawharanui Open Sanctuary Society Inc: www.tossi.org.nz

HUNUA RANGES REGIONAL PARK
HUNUA FALLS & COSSEYS DAM

Hunua Ranges is one of 22 regional parks managed by the Auckland Regional Council; a place of water reservoirs, podocarp–hardwood forests, and many enjoyable walks. Lying southeast of Auckland, the 14,000 hectare reserve is the largest tract of native forest remaining in the Auckland region and home to the most northerly population of North Island kokako.

Hunua Falls, one of the scenic highlights of the ranges is a popular place for swimming, picnicking and walking. This walk begins near the falls and follows the Massey and Wairoa Cosseys tracks to Cosseys Reservoir. From the reservoir the Cossey Gorge Track loops back to the carpark. Recently upgraded, the track is well-benched and gravelled, suiting walkers of moderate fitness and families with school-age children.

Hunua Falls to Cosseys Reservoir 1.5–2 hours

From the carpark a path leads to Hunua Falls, passing one of the 'masterpiece' frames which Auckland Regional Council have positioned in several of its better-known parks. The falls spill over an old basalt lava plug, with the pool at their base making a popular swimming spot.

Back at the carpark, cross the footbridge and follow the Cossey Gorge Track for 5–10 minutes through an avenue of tree ferns until the Massey Track branches off. Ascending steadily up a forested spur, the Massey Track climbs to 320 metres to intercept the Wairoa Cossey Track. Near the signposted track junction is a 5 minute loop track to some moderately sized kauri trees. Head left along the Wairoa Cossey Track, past a disappointing lookout over the Cosseys Reservoir. The track ends beside the reservoir, with views over the artificial lake created after construction of the earth and stone dam in the 1950s.

Cosseys Reservoir to Hunua Falls via Cossey Gorge Track 1 hour

From the reservoir, follow the Cossey Access Road for 5–10 minutes until signposts indicate the start of the Cossey Gorge Track. After a steep descent down a series of stairs, the track levels out somewhat to sidle beside the cascading waters of Cossey Creek. Northern rata, rewarewa and rimu protrude above a canopy consisting largely of tawa. After a 30–35 minute walk, ford the creek, which is rarely a problem to cross. A brief 5 minute climb along a fenceline leads up to the Massey Track turnoff, where it is just a 10 minute walk back to Hunua Falls.

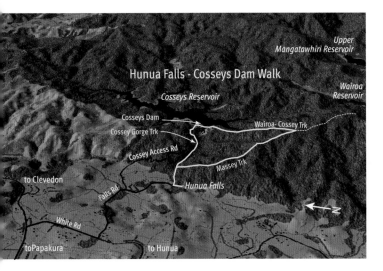

Grade Easy
Map S12 Maramarua
Total Walking Time 2.5–3 hours return
Access From Auckland, head south on SH 1 and take the Papakura off-ramp. Turn left and follow Beach Road across Great South Road and along Settlement Road. Turn right by Edmund Hillary School into Hunua Road. Falls Road branches off to end at a large carpark and picnic area. Allow an hour to drive from Auckland city.
Alternative route A shorter 30 minute loop walk, suitable for walkers of all abilities, passes two lookouts over Hunua Falls.
Information Auckland Regional Council Tel: 09-366-2000, www.arc.govt.nz

COROMANDEL PENINSULA
COROMANDEL WALKWAY

The Coromandel Walkway connects two of Coromandel's most scenic beaches – Fletcher and Stony bays – which occupy positions at the northern tip of the peninsula. Both bays, fringed by gnarled pohutukawa, have delightfully basic DOC campsites. The walkway itself passes through a mixture of farmland and native bush, offering fine views of the rugged coastline and distant Great Barrier Island. During late December the pohutukawa flowers a spectacular crimson, adding to the walkway's appeal. Although the track can be walked in either direction, generally the road to Fletcher Bay offers the best approach. From Coromandel allow for a long, winding drive, and take care on blind corners.

Fletcher Bay to Stony Bay 3–3.5 hours

From Fletcher Bay, the walkway climbs over farmland and above a bay overlooking Square Top Island and its adjacent reefs. After joining farm vehicle tracks, the walkway (marked by wooden posts) climbs up to a ridge overlooking the dramatic coastline around Sugar Loaf Rocks. A distant Cuvier Island is visible, as is Hauturu/Little Barrier Island.

After crossing a stile, the walkway enters forest, and soon begins a descent down to Poley Bay, reached about 1–1.5 hours from the track start. This narrow bay, with its strikingly layered volcanic cliffs, makes a pleasant place for swimming.

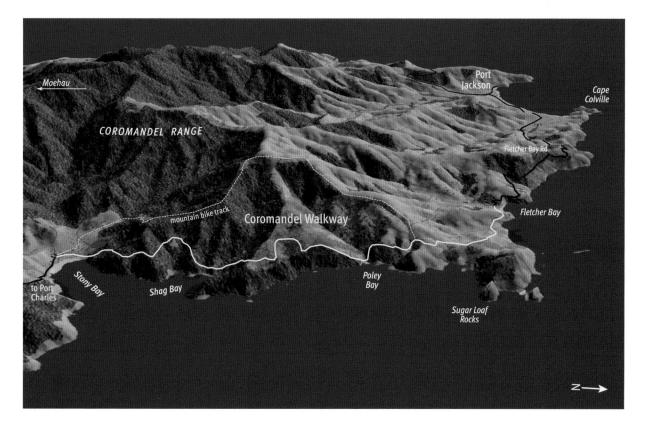

A steep climb out of Poley Bay leads to a high sidle track, which wends across forested slopes to where a short 5 minute side track reaches a superb viewpoint. Beyond, the walkway crosses numerous small gullies with occasional views of the coastline below. Around the final headland above Shag Bay, the track begins a zigzag down to Stony Bay, which offers good views of Mt Moehau, Coromandel's highest peak.

Stony Bay to Fletcher Bay via Mountain Bike Track 3.5–4 hours

From Stony Bay a round trip is possible by returning on the Mountain Bike Track, an old vehicle track that climbs significantly higher than the walkway itself. From the road end at Stony Bay, follow the old vehicle track across Stony Bay Creek and a tributary to begin an unrelenting 520 metre climb up the often-slippery track. Walkers might question why they are suffering such a gruelling ascent, but the views at the top are worth it. Port Jackson, Fletcher Bay, and the Coromandel coastline form the immediate foreground,

while Great Barrier Island somehow looks larger and closer than it did from the walkway. The track descends steadily over farmland, to rejoin the walkway near a dilapidated fencer's hut. Fletcher Bay is a further 30 minutes walk away.

Grade Medium

Maps S09 Colville, S10 Hauraki Gulf

Total Walking Time 6.5–7.5 hours return.

Access Reaching either end of the walkway involves winding gravel roads, and a night spent camping either side of your walk is recommended. To reach Fletcher Bay from Coromandel, take Colville Road past Colville to Whangaahei, where you turn off onto the Port Jackson Road. To reach Stony Bay, take the Port Charles Road from Whangaahei to Port Charles, then take the Stony Bay Road. Allow 90 minutes to drive to either bay from Coromandel. During summer, transport operators service the track.

Alternative route Walkers with less time will enjoy the walkway to Poley Bay and return (allow 2–3 hours return)

Information DOC Thames Tel: 07-867-9180

Walker above Fletcher Bay, Coromandel Walkway

COROMANDEL
KAURI LOOP WALK, WAITAWHETA VALLEY, KAIMAI–MAMAKU FOREST PARK • KARANGAHAKE GORGE HISTORIC WALKWAY, PAEROA

KAURI LOOP WALK, WAITAWHETA VALLEY, KAIMAI–MAMAKU FOREST PARK

The Waitawheta Valley drains the northern end of the Kaimai Range, which separates the Waikato from the Bay of Plenty. As recently as the 1920s, industrious loggers were hauling out kauri, using a tramway they had constructed up the valley. Fortunately, a small area of large kauri in a steep part of the valley escaped their attention, probably because they were too inaccessible to mill. This very enjoyable walk takes in a loop track through the kauri and ends on the recently excavated historic tramway. During summer, walkers can enjoy swimming in the sizeable Waitawheta River. The walk does involve two river crossings, both of which may be impassable after heavy rain.

Franklin Road to Kauri Trees 1.5–2 hours

From Franklin Road a track leads over farmland for 25–30 minutes to a gate marking the entrance to the forest park. Shortly afterward, take the signposted Kauri Loop Track that branches off to the left and soon crosses the Waitawheta River. On the far bank the track sidles briefly then begins a steady climb across forested slopes, crossing Trig Stream en route. More climbing and another sidle lead to a track junction. Ignore the track heading uphill (it leads to Ananui Falls and the Waitengaue valley) and head downhill. After a minute or two, you reach an impressive kauri, with a boardwalk around its base (for such sturdy and voluminous trees, kauri have surprisingly vulnerable roots). Another large kauri is nearby.

Kauri Trees to Waitawheta Valley and Franklin Road 1.5–2 hours

From the second kauri tree, the track descends sharply, often on a series of steps, through forest of a subtropical

Right A walker admires one of the remaining kauri, Kauri Loop Walkway.

nature. In places there are glimpses of the dark, foreboding cliffs of Bluff Stream. After 30 minutes the track ends where Bluff Stream merges into the main Waitawheta River. The best ford is upstream about 100 metres, where it is easy to access the Waitawheta Valley track.

From here to Franklin Road it is an easy stroll for an hour along the flat, historic tramway, with sections of recently excavated rail exposed and the original wooden sleepers still in place.

En route is a small waterfall, surrounded by a bank of parataniwha, and another track that branches off to Daly's Clearing and hut.

Grade Easy–Medium
Maps T13 Paeroa, Kaimai–Mamuku Forest Parkmap
Total Walking Time 3–4 hours
Access From SH 2, which runs through the Karangahake Gorge, take Waitawheta Road, turn into Spense Road, and then turn immediately into Franklin Road, where there is a carpark about 500 m from the road end.
Information DOC Tauranga Tel: 07-578-7677

KARANGAHAKE GORGE HISTORIC WALKWAY, PAEROA

During the heady days of New Zealand's gold rush, Karangahake was awash with people, machinery and gold. Several stamper batteries pounded quartz ore to extract the gold. And it was extracted in staggering quantities: during the peak of production in 1909, the Karangahake quartzfields boasted 60 per cent of New Zealand's gold output. This historic walkway sidles through a gorge on the Ohinemuri River, opposite SH 2 between Waikino and Karangahake. Part of the walkway follows a railway line closed in 1979, with both a tunnel and century-old trestle bridge offering plenty of interest to railway enthusiasts as well as walkers. En route numerous panels provide interesting information on the area's history, and the Waikino Visitor Centre is well worth visiting too. Well-benched and graded, the walkway is suitable for families and walkers of all abilities.

Karangahake to Trestle Bridge 20–25 minutes

From the carpark, a large suspension bridge crosses the Ohinemuri River just downstream of its confluence with the Waitawheta River to reach the main walkway. Head

The main walkway beside the Ohinemuri River, Karangahake Gorge Historic Walkway

upstream, and cross a second footbridge (which offers good views up the Waitawheta River) to reach the Woodstock Battery and a track junction. Here the worthwhile Windows Walk branches off past the Talisman Battery site (40 minutes return).

The main walkway continues upstream, sidling beside the Ohinemuri River as it passes through a gorge. While traffic noise from SH 2 (on the opposite side of the river) reduces the peace, it was probably more industrial when the valley resounded to the thump of stamper batteries. The track hugs the banks of the gorge, through which the Ohinemuri tumbles over boulder jumbles, until it reaches a trestle bridge (built in 1905) across the river. Don't cross yet: you'll return to Karangahake that way.

Trestle Bridge to Waikino via Owharoa Falls
75–90 minutes each way (note that mountain bikes are permitted on this section)

Continuing up the valley, the track widens considerably as it follows the line of the old railway, built between 1900 and 1905 to service the mines. Now above the gorge, the Ohinemuri is more subdued. Easy walking for another 25–30 minutes leads to a side track to a thin waterfall and quarry site (5 minutes return). Walk for another 15–20 minutes to Waitawheta Road, where a short 3 minute side track leads to the Owharoa Falls. After another 25–30 minutes walking upvalley, the track reaches the Victoria Battery Site. Here, considerable time can be spent exploring the concrete foundations of what was once New Zealand's largest ore crushing plant, boasting 200 stampers, each capable of crushing 4 tons of ore daily. The plant processed ore from Waihi's Martha Mine, and finally closed in 1955 after 58 years of

Trestle Bridge (built 1905) with the tunnel beyond formed part of the railway line that was closed in 1971

activity. Beyond the site, another 10 minutes walking leads across a footbridge over the Ohinemuri River to the Waikino Railway Station and Visitor Centre and the end of the track. Return back along the track to the Trestle Bridge.

Trestle Bridge to Karangahake via Tunnel and Crown Battery Site 25–30 minutes

Cross the Trestle Bridge and enter the kilometre long railway tunnel, lit dimly with overhead lights (you may want to take a torch as well). Lights notwithstanding, the tunnel can be eerily dark; water drips, voices echo and the far end takes a while to reach. Beyond the tunnel exit, an overbridge crosses SH 2 and the Ohinemuri River in quick succession, to reach the crumbling brick remains of the Crown Battery (closed in 1916). From here, follow the walkway upstream for 15 minutes and cross the footbridge back to the main Karangahake carpark.

Grade Easy–Medium
Maps T13 Paeroa
Total Walking Time 3.5–4 hours return
Access Karangahake lies between Paeroa and Waihi off SH 2. A large carpark with shelters, toilets and information panels is signposted just off the highway.
Alternative route Myriad other walking possibilities exist in the area. Walkers wanting a shorter option will enjoy the Karangahake Tunnel Loop Walk (follow the walkway as far as the Trestle Bridge and return via the tunnel and Crown Battery – a 45–60 minute loop). Alternatively, an excellent 3–4 hour loop track – suitable for fitter walkers – exists up the Waitawheta Gorge (using the Crown, Dubbo 96 Number 7 Level and Scotsman Gully tracks), accessible from the Karangahake carpark.
Information DOC Tauranga Tel: 07-349-7400
Email: bayofplenty@doc.govt.nz

COROMANDEL FOREST PARK
KAUAERANGA KAURI TRAIL

By the 1920s, kauri logging was well past its heyday, with all but the most inaccessible kauri trees long since converted into timber for the houses of Auckland, Melbourne and San Francisco. However in the remote, steep volcanic terrain of the Coromandel Range, loggers enjoyed one last frenzy of activity, using ingenious dams to literally flush logs out of the mountains. One of New Zealand's best-preserved kauri dams forms the central attraction of this increasingly popular track, known as the Kauaeranga Kauri Trail. Many trampers walk the trail over 2 days, staying at Pinnacles Hut en route. But reasonably fit walkers can enjoy the track over the course of a full day.

Road End to Hydro Camp via Webb Creek
1.5–2 hours
From the road end, the well-graded track crosses the Ka-uaeranga River on a swingbridge, before beginning a steady climb up beside Webb Creek, passing some attractive falls and crossing a few footbridges en route. After about 2 hours, the track reaches the Hydro Camp, a base used by workers erecting powerlines over the range in the 1940s. From here, take the signposted route towards Pinnacles Hut.

Hydro Camp to Pinnacles Hut (80 bunks, gas cooking rings, solar lighting) 40–60 minutes
From the Hydro Camp the track passes through more regenerating kauri forest, eventually cresting the broad tops of the Coromandel Range to reach Pinnacles Hut, New Zealand's largest. A 5 minute side track leads to the partially restored Dancing Camp dam (built in 1924), the second largest of around 100 kauri dams that were constructed in the valley in the 1920s.

Walkers at Dancing Camp kauri dam

The Pinnacles
Pinnacles Hut
Dancing Camp Dam
Kauaeranga Kauri Trail
Hydro Camp
Billy Goat Basin
Billy Goat Falls
Billy Goat Track
Table Mountain
Kauaeranga River
Trestle View campground
Kauaeranga Valley Road to Thames
to Tarawaere carpark
Tairua River

Hydro Camp to Road End via Billy Goat Track
2–3 hours

Back at the Hydro Camp, the Kauri Trail continues on past a clearing to Billy Goat Basin. At a track junction beyond the clearing, take the Billy Goat Track. This leads past a viewpoint of the 180 metre Billy Goat Falls, over which many kauri logs were wastefully smashed before construction of the 'Billy Goat Incline' tramway. At a restored section of the tramway, walkers can imagine the steam haulers that were used to lower kauri logs down to the valley to circumvent the destructive falls. The track gradient eases lower down, and crosses a swingbridge over the Kauaeranga River to the Tarawaere carpark.

Grade Medium–Hard
Map T12 Thames
Total Walking Time 5–7 hours round trip
Access Turn off SH 25 onto the Kauaeranga Valley Road, 2 km south of Thames. Follow the road for 21 km to the road end at the Trestle View campground.
Alternative route The section from the Hydro Camp to Pinnacles Hut and the Dancing Camp dam can be omitted to shorten the track by 1.5–2 hours.
Information DOC Thames Tel: 07-867-9180

Opposite Wairere Falls, Kaimai Mamuku Forest Park

KAIMAI–MAMAKU FOREST PARK
WAIRERE FALLS

Wairere Falls, the highest in Kaimai–Mamaku Forest Park, tumble in two thin columns over a sharp escarpment of the Kaimai Range, with a total fall of 153 metres. This track, beginning near Matamata in the Waikato, leads to a lookout at the base of the falls on a well-developed walking track suitable for families with school-age children. Fitter walkers may like to use a tramping track that climbs stiffly onto the Kaimai Range to a viewpoint at the top of the falls.

Goodwin Road to Wairere Falls Lookout
45–60 minutes

From the carpark a well-formed and gravelled track soon leads into bush and shortly reaches the Wairere Stream. The track weaves amongst mossy boulders, with footbridges spanning the stream at three points. Further up, as the Wairere narrows into a gorge, a series of stairs leads steeply around a cliff, up to a grove where subtropical trees dominate: nikau, kohekohe and puriri. Shortly beyond, a wooden viewing platform provides a fine view of the falls.

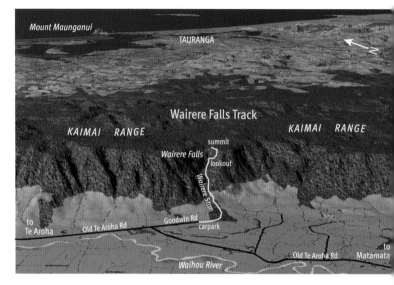

Lookout to Wairere Falls Summit 45–60 minutes

From the lookout a rougher track climbs towards the Kaimai Range, following the route of an old Maori trail that connected the Bay of Plenty and the Waikato. More sections of stairs lead steeply upwards and the gradient does not ease until the track approaches the range crest. There a side trail leads to a viewing platform providing a giddy view down the falls, and a broad panorama of the Waikato's patchwork quilt plains.

Grade Easy (falls lookout), Medium (falls summit)
Maps T14 Morrinsville, Kaimai–Mamaku Forest Parkmap
Total Walking Time 1.5–2 hours return (lookout), 3–4 hours return (top of falls)
Access From SH 27, just north of Waharoa, take Wardville and Armadale roads to Gordon. From Gordon, take the old Te Aroha Road for 5 km until Goodwin Road branches off. Goodwin Road ends after 1 km at the Wairere Falls carpark (toilets available). Alternatively, from the township of Te Aroha, take the Te Aroha–Gordon Road to Gordon.
Information DOC Hamilton Tel: 07-838-3363

KING COUNTRY
TAWARAU FOREST

Among walkers, the layered limestone cliffs of Paparoa National Park are justly famous. Few, however, know that a North Island version exists in the Mangaohae Valley of the King Country's Tawarau Forest. Two worthwhile walks in Tawarau Forest are described here.

Loop Track and Tawarau Falls 2.5–3 hours return

The Loop Track is a 2–3 hour round trip that passes through intriguing limestone bluffs and lush forest to reach the Tawarau Falls. From Appletree Road, a vehicle track climbs through pine forest for a short distance before dropping into the Tawarau Valley, fording the river twice en route.

After the second ford, the track reaches a junction, where the loop track ends. Head left, fording the Tawarau River twice more before a side trail leads to the falls themselves. Beyond, the track loop continues through more pines into a section of native forest to regain the junction.

Gorge Track 3.5–4 hours one way

The Gorge Track begins from a farmhouse at Mangaohae, and ends at Speedies Road, off the main Te Anga Road. The through trip takes about 3.5–4 hours, and requires a car juggle. Alternatively, Blackberry Flat or the Bullring Track junction make turnaround points.

Limestone formations, Mangaohae Stream, Tawarau Forest

From Mangaohae, the first section crosses private farmland, and permission should be sought with the farmer. After about 20 minutes of sometimes boggy walking over the farmland, the track enters luxuriant forest and follows the true right bank of the Mangaohae Stream. For the next 90 minutes the track follows the route of an old coach trail on an easy gradient, often right beneath spectacular layered bluffs. Shortly before reaching a track junction, the Mangaohae merges with the Tawarau River. At the junction stay on the true left – the Bullring Track branches off, crossing the Tawarau River on a footbridge. After a further 15 minutes the track reaches the Blackberry Flat campsite, set in a small grassy clearing. Forty-five minutes beyond the flat, the terrain opens out into farmland and continues on to reach Speedies Road after another 45 minutes.

Grade Easy (Loop Track), Medium (Gorge Track)
Map R16 Marokopa
Total Walking Time Loop Track, 2.5–3 hours (round trip); Gorge Track, 7–8 hours return, or 5 hours return to Blackberry Flat.
Access Both Appletree (access to Loop Track) and Speedies (end of Gorge Track) roads branch off Te Anga Road, the main road between Te Kuiti and Marokopa. The start of the Gorge Track begins from Were Road, reached from just north of Te Kuiti on Oparure and Ngapaenga roads.
Alternative route The Bullring Route connects Loop Track and Gorge Track, and also offers access to Double Falls.
Information DOC Te Kuiti Tel: 07-878-1050

PIRONGIA FOREST PARK
MANGAKARA NATURE WALK & RUAPANAE

Mt Pirongia, an old extinct volcano, is the highest mountain in the Waikato and the central feature of Pirongia Forest Park. Botanically, Pirongia's location is interesting because it marks the transition between the warm-loving kauri forests of the north and the beech and podocarp–beech forests of the south. The park's latitude is the naturally occurring southern limit for species such as kauri and mangeao.

Families or walkers who prefer a short walk can enjoy the well-benched Mangakara Nature Walk, which carves a loop through some of the park's lushest forest. From the Nature Walk, walkers can use the Ruapanae and Tirohanga tracks to reach Ruapanae, a significant rocky knoll with excellent views of Hamilton and the Waikato basin.

Pirongia Forest Park Lodge and Mangakara Nature Walk 1 hour return

From the Grey Road carpark, the well-benched and gravelled Mangakara Nature Walk sidles through lush forest

Dappled light in tawa forest, Ruapanae Track

down to the loop track that circles around the photogenic Mangakara Stream, crossing two footbridges en route. Rimu and kahikatea, tawa, kohekohe and nikau palms dominate.

Mangakara Stream to Ruapanae 1.5 hours

Near the footbridge at the upstream end of Mangakara Stream, a signposted trail indicates the turnoff to the Ruapanae Track. The Ruapanae Track is reached shortly afterward; head left, as the right branch goes to Waite Road. An hour climbing gently along the Ruapanae Track, passing through some fine stand of tawa forest, leads to the Tirohanga Track. A short, steep climb ensues up to the summit of Ruapanae (723 m). Either return to Grey Road, or – a shorter option – exit to Corcoran Road.

Grade Easy (Mangakara Nature Walk), Medium (Ruapanae)
Map Te Awamutu S15
Total Walking Time 5 hours return (Ruapanae)
Access From Pirongia drive north for 5 km, turn left onto Bridge Road, then left onto Hodgson Road after 1 km, and finally left again onto Grey Road. At the road end, there are toilets, a carpark, information shelter and the Pirongia Forest Park Lodge.
Alternative route Ambitious walkers can continue on to the summit of Mt Pirongia and return over the Mahaukura Track to Grey Road. This is for fit and experienced trampers only (allow 8–11 hours).
Information DOC Hamilton Tel: 07-838-3363

PIRONGIA FOREST PARK
TE TOTO GORGE & MT KARIOI

Karioi, the sentinel of Raglan Harbour, is a modest 756 metre mountain perched above the Tasman Sea. The mountain and its cloak of forests are an outlier of Pirongia Forest Park, and form the only coast-to-mountaintop sequence of forest remaining anywhere between Auckland and the northern King Country.

Mt Karioi is one of several extinct volcanoes (the others are Mt Pirongia, Kakepuku and Te Kawa) that form an arc from the coast at Raglan to inland near Te Awamutu. Karioi was formed between 2.9 and 2.16 million years ago when molten rock, mainly basalt and andesite, erupted from the subduction zone some 250 kilometres below the earth's surface. Since then wind and water have eroded the extinct volcano to its present height and shape.

The two walks here can be combined in a full but enjoyable 'sea to summit' day, or tackled separately. Both are of tramping track standard and will require good fitness and footwear.

Mt Karioi Track to Summit 3–3.5 hours

Although steeper and more strenuous, this track is the more dramatic of the two that reach the summit of Mt Karioi (the alternative Wairake Track approaches the summit from farmland on the mountain's southern side). From the carpark the track climbs abruptly through a manuka stand, following a fenceline up a spur across retired farmland. Further up, the track enters forest, and continues to climb stiffly until breaching a knoll, where there is a view of the wind-sheared flanks of the upper mountain. After a brief descent, including a section down a ladder, the track climbs very steeply, with fixed chains to aid progress.

After 2 hours or more from the carpark, the track surmounts the first prominent knoll on the summit ridge at 706 metres. A 5 minute side track leads to an excellent viewpoint of Raglan Harbour.

Walkers can choose to turn around here, or continue on to the main summit about an undulating hour further on. *Dracophyllum latifolium*, *Quintinia* and kamahi dominate the stunted vegetation, with the occasional miro too. A knoll atop a narrow ridge is reached about 15 minutes before the actual summit, which sports a telecommunications aerial. There are expansive views over Mt Pirongia, Raglan, Aotea

Mangakara Stream,
Pirongia Forest Park

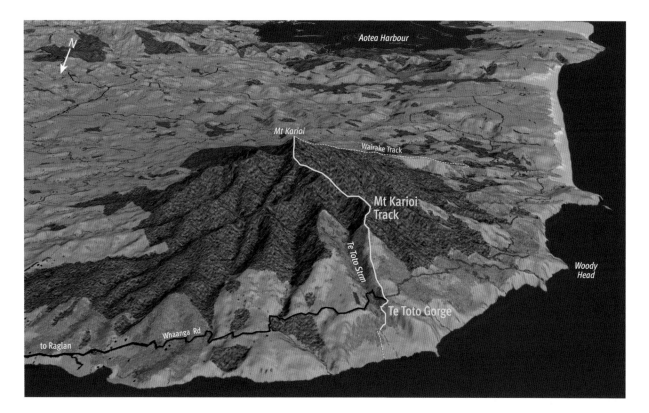

and Kawhia harbours, as well as the more distant peaks of Maungatautari, Te Aroha, Pureora and – on a very clear day – even Mt Taranaki.

Te Toto Gorge Walk 1 hour return

The land surrounding Te Toto Gorge was added to Pirongia Forest Park in 1998. A place of eerie cliffs and lush vegetation, the gorge has a rather gruesome history. A number of Maori slaves – including women and children – were pushed to their death over the edge here. From a wooden viewing platform near the carpark, walkers gain the sort of view that can induce vertigo in even the staunchest.

From the carpark the track descends steeply through coastal forest including kohekohe, kawakawa and karaka – the latter most likely planted by Maori as a food source. After about 15 minutes the gradient eases and the track reaches Te Toto Stream. The marked track ends here, but it is simple enough to push through open grassy vegetation

for another 15 minutes to the bouldery shoreline. Looking back gives walkers a fine view of the cliffs.

Grade Easy (Te Toto Gorge), Hard (Mt Karioi)
Map R14 Raglan
Total Walking Time Te Toto Gorge and Karioi summit return 6–8 hours
Access From Hamilton take SH 23 to Raglan. From the main street of town take Wainui Road which winds toward Karioi, and turns into Whaanga Road. The Te Toto Gorge carpark is well signposted.
Alternative route For those who can arrange the transport, a traverse of Mt Karioi ascending the Mt Karioi Track and descending the Wairake Track is an attractive option. Allow 7–8 hours for the through trip.
Information DOC Hamilton Tel: 07-838-3363

PUREORA FOREST PARK
MT PUREORA

Mt Pureora is probably the most accessible summit of any national or forest park in New Zealand. The mountain's volcanic origins are obvious in its cone shape, but its flattened nature and modest height suggest a long period of dormancy.

Mt Pureora's summit has a small patch of subalpine plants (winter snowfalls are rare but not unknown) and fine 360 degree views over a great swathe of country, including Lake Taupo, the Kaimanawa and Hauhungaroa ranges, Tongariro National Park, and closer at hand, the craggy summit of Mt Titiraupenga. On exceptionally clear days the distant summits of Mt Taranaki and Maungatautari sometimes shoulder into view.

Although uphill all the way (a 340 metre ascent), school-age children should experience no undue difficulties with the walk, and anyone of modest fitness can reach the top. It's a great place to observe the altitudinal stratification of a mountainside forest, which ranges from mature podocarp forest to stunted subalpine shrubs.

Carpark to Pureora Summit 1–1.5 hours

From Link Road the track begins a gradual climb through forest dominated by stately rimu. Higher up, totara and hinau become more common. The climb gradually steepens, crossing two small streams (one bridged), and the totara becomes increasingly stunted. The track now has large sections of boardwalk, put in to protect the fragile volcanic soils. Through subalpine scrub the track breaks out onto the open top to reach the trig station. Walkers with botanical inclinations will notice broadleaf, stinkwood, mountain holly, *Gaultheria*, *Lycopodium*, and a species of *Brachyglottis*. During summer prolific everlasting daisies add delicate colour to the summit.

Grade Easy–Medium
Map T17 Whakamaru
Total Walking Time 2–2.5 hours return
Access Mt Pureora is reached from a small carpark on Link Road, a gravel road connecting SH 32 (the Western Bays road) with SH 30 (between Te Kuiti and Mangakino). The track start is signposted about 12 km from Pureora Village. Pureora Village has cabins for hire, a nearby camping area and a multitude of good short walks, ranging from 10 minutes to half a day. Worth visiting is the forest tower, site of an infamous 1978 tree-top occupation by conservationist Stephen King and others, who were protesting against NZ Forest Service logging in the area.
Alternative route From the summit of Mt Pureora the Toitoi track provides an alternative descent route, leading down to a side road off Link Road. This option requires alternative transport arrangements, as the tracks end at roads 13 km apart.
Information DOC Pureora Tel: 07-386-8607, Email: pureorafc@doc.govt.nz

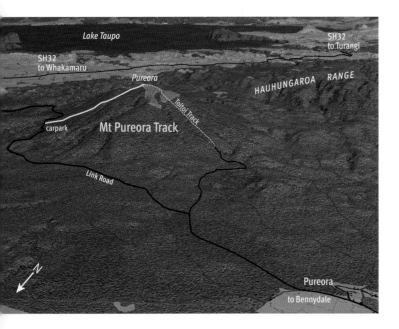

Lake Taupo
SH32 to Turangi
SH32 to Whakamaru
Pureora
HAUHUNGAROA RANGE
Toitoi Track
carpark
Mt Pureora Track
Link Road
Pureora to Bennydale

Opposite *Dawn at Cook's Cove*

EAST COAST
COOK'S COVE WALKWAY

Cook's Cove is named after Captain James Cook, who visited the area during October 1769. At Tolaga Bay, Cook replenished his supplies, traded with local Maori, and made repairs to his ship, the Endeavour. *At Cook's Cove itself, his crew collected fresh water and were much taken by the landscape, particularly the coastal formation known as the Hole in the Wall, or Te Kotere o te Whenua.*

Lying just south of Tolaga Bay, the DOC-managed walkway crosses private farmland to reach Cook's Cove. It is suitable for walkers of all abilities. Note that during the spring lambing season (late winter to the end of Labour weekend), the walkway is not open, and can also be closed at other times due to high fire risk. Carry your own water.

Wharf Road Carpark to Cook's Cove
60–75 minutes

From the carpark, the walkway passes through a gate with an information panel, and begins a climb through patches of open kanuka up onto farmland studded with cabbage trees. Yellow marker posts indicate the route.

After 20–30 minutes the walkway reaches a wooden platform overlooking Cook's Cove. From the lookout, a descent down a series of stairs zigzags through regenerating forest. Soon after crossing a footbridge, the track reaches a signposted junction on the edge of grassy flats (a longdrop

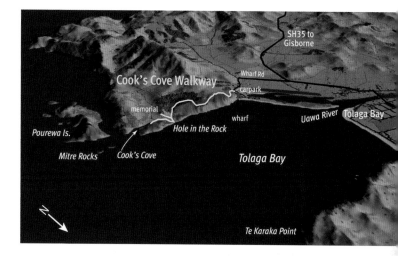

toilet is nearby). Head right up grassy slopes for 10 minutes to reach a concrete memorial to Cook, which offers perhaps the best view of the cove, framed by Mitre Rocks.

Back at the junction, head left for 5 minutes to reach the interesting Hole in the Rock, a natural archway through which you can walk to a pleasant rocky beach. Prominent in the foreground view is the Tolaga Bay wharf (built in 1925–29) – possibly the longest in the Southern Hemisphere, and certainly in New Zealand. Back at the junction again, cross the flats to reach the tidal head of Cook's Cove. Animal trails lead to a headland where Mitre Rocks and the crumbly cliffs of Pourewa Island are prominent.

Grade Easy
Map Z17 Tolaga Bay
Total Walking Time 2–2.5 hours return
Access Drive to Tolaga Bay on SH 35, 54 km north of Gisborne. Two km south of Tolaga Bay township, at the southern end of the bay, turn off onto Wharf Road. An overflow carpark is available at the beach nearby next to the motor camp.
Information DOC Gisborne Tel: 06-869-0460

TE UREWERA NATIONAL PARK
LAKE WAIKAREITI

Although much smaller than its neighbour Waikaremoana, Lake Waikareiti offers walkers a more intimate experience; instead of the almost ocean-like tempestuousness of the larger lake, with its domineering bluffs, Waikareiti has quieter, island-studded waters flanked by overhanging forest. The lake lies in the heart of Te Urewera National Park, the largest in the North Island, where birdlife is generally good.

There are several options for walks here. Families and those short on time can enjoy the simple stroll up a well-benched track to the lake edge. Those wanting a longer loop trip can take in the interesting wetlands of the Ruapani Track. And the hut at Sandy Bay (on the far shore of the lake) makes a worthwhile destination in itself, although this involves a longer day, and is not a loop.

Evening, Lake Waikareiti

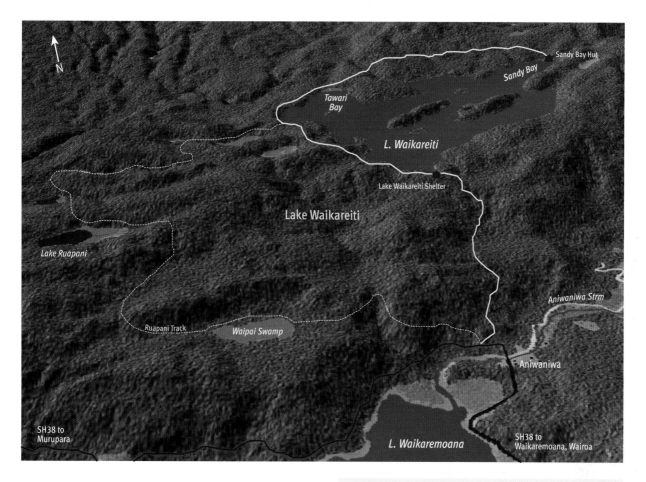

Aniwaniwa to Lake Waikareiti Shelter 1 hour

The well-benched and graded track climbs slowly through dense forest, crossing a number of small streams on footbridges. After cresting a lip, the track reaches the lake edge, where a basic shelter offers respite from the elements if they prove inclement.

Shelter to Sandy Bay Hut (18 bunks, gas heater, $20/night) 2–3 hours

From the shelter, the Lake Waikareiti Track sidles away from the lake, and past the turnoff to the Ruapani Track. At Tawari Bay the track skirts the lake edge again, with views of the islands. Beyond, an extensive sidle strikes inland, and the lake remains out of view until Sandy Bay.

Grade Medium
Maps W18 Waikaremoana, Urewera Parkmap
Total Walking Time 5–7 hours
Access Between SH 5, (south of Rotorua) and SH 2 (near Wairoa), SH 38 crosses through Te Urewera National Park to reach Lake Waikaremoana. At Waikaremoana village is a motorcamp and shop, and at nearby Aniwaniwa is the DOC visitor centre offering information and toilets.
Alternative route The 5–6 hour Ruapani Track offers trampers an alternative – although longer way – to tramp back to Aniwaniwa from the Lake Waikareiti shelter. It branches off the main track near Tawari Bay.
Information DOC Aniwaniwa Tel: 06-837-3803

WHIRINAKI FOREST PARK
ARAHAKI LAGOON & TE WHAITI NUI A TOI CANYON

Whirinaki Forest Park, accessible off SH 38 near Murupara, is famed for its podocarp forests – arguably the finest in the country. Podocarps, including rimu, kahikatea, totara, miro and matai, certainly occur in a density rarely encountered elsewhere, forming a unique glimpse of the type of forests that once dominated Gondwana some 150 million years ago. The park offers a range of very good walks, but perhaps the best are these two, which together can easily be accomplished over the course of a leisurely day. Well-benched and graded, both tracks suit families and walkers of all abilities.

Arahaki Carpark to Arahaki Lagoon 1-1.5 hours

Arahaki Lagoon, a small wetland surrounded by elegant kahikatea forest, is one the highlights of Whirinaki Forest Park. From the road end, the track descends almost immediately to a footbridge over the Waiatiu Stream, then sidles gently onto an undulating bush terrace boasting fine podocarp–hardwood forest, with mature matai and miro the most noticeable emergent trees. Stands of tawa dominate other areas.

After 60–90 minutes the track ends at a small arm of the

Kahikatea forest, Arahaki lagoon

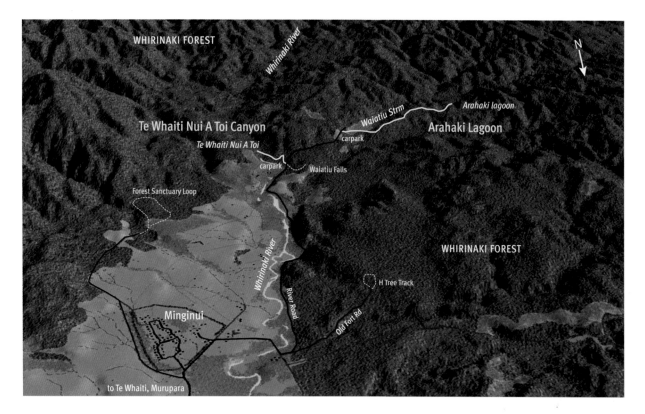

lagoon. Heavy rain causes the lagoon to expand into the surrounding forest, making a scene of exquisite reflections. During dry periods the lagoon shrinks markedly, exposing aquatic foliage (largely sedges) and the buttresses of the kahikatea trees.

Whirinaki Carpark to top of Te Whaiti Nui A Toi Canyon 20–30 minutes

A well-benched and graded track leads through a fine section of forest dominated by all five of the major podocarp species. After about 10–15 minutes the track reaches a footbridge over the sizeable Whirinaki River. The footbridge provides a good view of Te Whaiti Nui A Toi canyon, a slot gorge with distinctively angular ignimbrite columns and vibrant mosses. Upstream, walkers can continue along the Whirinaki Track, following terraces on the true right of the river for another 10–15 minutes to a viewpoint where the gorge opens out. Blue duck sometimes frequent the river here.

Grade Easy

Map V18 Whirinaki

Total Walking Time Arahaki Lagoon, 2–3 hours return; Te Whaiti Nui a Toi Canyon, 40–60 minutes return

Access Access is from SH 38, 18 km east of Murupara, where a signposted turnoff directs you towards the town of Minginui. Don't go into the town, but turn right, across a bridge over the Whirinaki River, and then turn left onto River Road. The track to the canyon begins at the main Whirinaki carpark, while the track to Arahaki Lagoon branches off at the end of the formed road, a kilometre further on.

Alternative route Other worthwhile short walks in the area are The H-Tree track, the Waiatiu Falls track, and Forest Sanctuary loop.

Information DOC Murupara Tel: 07-366-1080

ROTORUA
TARAWERA FALLS & LAKE TARAWERA •
LAKE OKATAINA SCENIC RESERVE

TARAWERA FALLS AND LAKE TARAWERA

The 65 metre Tarawera Falls erupt from a fissure in an impressive rhyolitic cliff, an explosion of water that is perhaps unique in New Zealand, certainly in the Bay of Plenty. The cliffs themselves resulted after a rhyolitic lava flow, erupting from nearby Mt Tarawera some 11,000 years ago, abruptly ended. Adding interest to the area is the unusual mixture of rata and pohutukawa, the latter normally associated with coastal areas. The two Metrosideros species have interbred to produce hybrid specimens with varying leaf shapes. From the falls, the Northern Tarawera Track leads to the shores of Lake Tarawera at Te Tapahoro Bay.

Road access to Tarawera Falls is from Kawerau through a private plantation forest, and a permit must be obtained from the Visitor Information Centre (Tel: 07-323-7550) on the day of your intended trip. Permits cost $3.50 per vehicle.

Carpark to Tarawera Falls 20 minutes

From the carpark, a well-developed, easy track leads upstream on the true right of the Tarawera River for 10 minutes before crossing a footbridge to the true left. Another 10 minute walk upstream leads to a viewing area of the falls.

Tarawera Falls to Te Tapahoro Bay 1.5 hours

Beyond the falls, the track climbs stiffly to reach a point above the falls. Here, a signposted track junction offers a shortcut that will save 10 minutes walking, but the more scenic option is to take the track that follows the Tarawera River. The dazzlingly clear blue river alternates between cascades and tranquil pools, and at one point boils down into an underground passage.

The wide, easy track remains on the true left of the river all the way to Te Tapahoro Bay, passing through sections of manuka and rata forest that have regenerated since the mighty Tarawera eruption of 1886. Where the Tarawera River issues from the voluminous Lake Tarawera, a wooden footbridge leads across to a popular campsite at Te Tapahoro

Bay, which is accessible from boat or road. It is worth continuing on for another 5 minutes along the North Tarawera Track to a jetty which has fine views over the lake, with Mt Tarawera brooding above.

> **Grade** Easy–Medium
> **Map** V16 Kawerau
> **Total Walking Time** 4–5 hours return
> **Access** From Kawerau, turn off Tamarangi Drive into Islington Street, then right onto Onslow Street, left onto Fenton Street, right onto River Road and left onto Waterhouse Street. From there private forest roads are followed: Tarawera Road, Fenton Mill Road and finally left onto Waterfall Road. In total it is 25 km from Kawerau or 30 minutes drive, mainly on gravel roads.
> **Alternative route** For those with boat or sea kayak access, Tarawera Falls can be reached from the camping area at Te Tapahoro Bay on Lake Tarawera. Another option is the link with the Eastern Okataina Walkway (see Lake Okataina walk).
> **Information** DOC Rotorua Tel: 07-366-1080

LAKE OKATAINA SCENIC RESERVE

Of all Rotorua's numerous lakes, Okataina is arguably the most attractive; it's certainly the one in the most pristine condition. The deep lake was formerly an arm of Lake Tarawera until about 7000 years ago, when a lava dome erupted in the vicinity of what is now Humphries Bay, separating the two lakes.

In times past the lake formed an important part of the waterways used by local Maori as transport routes. Maori portaged their waka (canoes) over a narrow isthmus separating Lakes Okataina and Tarawera, still a possibility for modern-day sea kayakers.

In an act of considerable generosity, local iwi Ngati Tarawhai gifted the lakeshores to the Crown in 1921, forming the basis for the scenic reserve. Their people had occupied the area for hundreds of years, with their main pa at Te Koutu Point.

Two walkways pass through the forests surrounding Lake Okataina, but the shorter and more scenic of the two is the Eastern Okataina Walkway. This follows the eastern flanks of the lake and crosses the isthmus to Humphries Bay, on neighbouring Lake Tarawera, with swimming opportunities at both lakes. The Humphries Bay camping area offers possibilities for those wanting an overnight tramp. From the bay, walkers need to either arrange a water taxi on Lake Tarawera, or return back to the Okataina carpark.

Okataina Carpark to Humphries Bay 2.5–3 hours

The well-marked track initially follows close to the eastern shores of Lake Okataina, soon passing a large natural amphitheatre known as the Soundshell. Shortly beyond, a 5 minute side track leads to the historic pa site on Te Koutu Point. After about 30–40 minutes, the track reaches Kaiwaka Bay and there turns inland for an hour of undulating travel through dense forest dominated by tawa before reaching the lake once again. Beyond here the track sidles about 10 metres above the lake for another 30 minutes, before reaching the south end of the lake at Otangimoana Bay.

Here the track strikes inland over the isthmus, reaching Humphries Bay after a further 20 minutes. Humphries Bay has toilets and a small camping area, which is reserved for overnight trampers or kayakers. It overlooks Lake Tarawera and Mt Tarawera beyond.

Grade Easy–Medium
Map V16 Tarawera
Total Walking Time Okataina carpark to Humphries Bay 5.5–6 hours return.
Access Lake Okataina Road branches off SH 30, approximately 20 km from Rotorua. The 6 km road ends at a carpark where there is a lodge, picnic area, toilets, shelter, information panels and jetty.
Alternative route From Humphries Bay walkers can join the Northern Tarawera Track, which follows the shores of Lake Tarawera to Tapahoro Bay (see Tarawera Falls walk). This is a through route only, and would take a full day of some 6–8 hours.
Information DOC Rotorua Tel: 07-366-1080

TONGARIRO NATIONAL PARK
TONGARIRO ALPINE CROSSING

Ketetahi Springs from the Tongariro Alpine Crossing Track

In recent decades the Tongariro Alpine Crossing has begun to attract the epithet of 'New Zealand's best day tramp', a judgement that multitudes have voted for with their feet. Certainly the track crosses remarkable and vividly colourful volcanic landscapes with outstanding views and two good huts en route. And for sheer diversity the Tongariro Alpine Crossing is hard to beat, traversing the forests below Ketetahi, the lunar terrain of Central Crater, the dazzling blue–green of the Emerald Lakes, the steaming, sulphurous vent of Red Crater, and the bubbling Mangatepopo Stream with its curious statue-like lava formations.

Walkers, however, need to be mentally prepared to be part of a people train: on a fine day, literally hundreds walk the Tongariro Alpine Crossing. Many are woefully under-prepared. Take warm, weatherproof clothing as the weather can change extremely rapidly, and between huts the terrain is very exposed. During winter, an ice axe and crampons are often essential. Although there are streams en route, these are probably not safe for drinking, so carry plenty of water and fill up at hut water tanks.

Road End to Ketetahi Hut (26 bunks, gas cookers, gas heaters) 2–3 hours

From the carpark the well-gravelled track climbs gradually through podocarp–hardwood forest, crossing a footbridge en route. Above the bushline, the steam from Ketetahi Springs becomes visible. Poles lead over gentle tussock slopes, and then the track steepens as it bypasses the springs (this is private land, no trespassing). Across some incised scoria gullies, the trail sidles to Ketetahi Hut, which has commanding views of Lake Rotoaira, Mt Pihanga, Lake Taupo and the Kaimanawa Mountains.

Ketetahi Hut to Mangatepopo Hut (26 bunks, gas cookers, gas heaters) 4–5.5 hours

Beyond Ketetahi Hut, the trail climbs and sidles into Central Crater, a large flat depression, with Blue Lake nearby. Poles lead across the crater and down to the Emerald Lakes, three old explosion pits now filled by highly acidic waters of vivid colours.

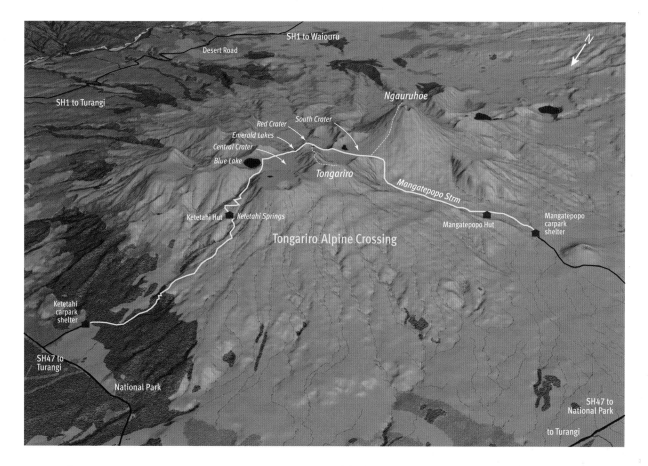

A well-worn scramble up a scree slope leads to a ridge overlooking Red Crater, with excellent views. From this high point of the track (1886 m) are grand views of Ruapehu, partially obscured behind Ngauruhoe and any number of surrounding hills and mountains. Westwards a side trail leads to the summit of Tongariro (1967 m) – allow an extra 2 hours return.

Poles lead down a steepish slope into South Crater, and over to the lip above the Mangatepopo Valley. Keen and appropriately equipped walkers sometimes tackle an ascent of Ngauruhoe (2287 m) from here (allow an extra 3 hours return). The main trail zigzags down sharp slopes to the Mangatepopo Valley (toilets available here) and along flat terrain beside old lava flows. Mangatepopo Hut is just 20 minutes from the road end.

Grade Medium–Hard

Maps T19 Tongariro, Tongariro Parkmap

Total Walking Time 6–8 hours one way

Access From Turangi drive south on SH 1 for 10 km, then turn off onto SH 47. The small gravel side road to the Ketetahi carpark branches off on the left after about 15 km. Many transport operators will arrange a drop off and pick up.

Alternative route Shorter sections of the track are enjoyable for those who don't want to walk the whole crossing. Red Crater is about the halfway point; shorter turnaround landmarks are Blue Lake (from the Ketetahi end) or South Crater (from the Mangatepopo end).

Information DOC Whakapapa Tel: 07-892-3729

TONGARIRO NATIONAL PARK
TAMA LAKES & TARANAKI FALLS

The sizeable Tama Lakes occupy old, deep explosion craters on the southern side of Mt Ngauruhoe, blue oases in an otherwise quite desolate, barren topography. From Whakapapa Village this worthwhile day trip follows part of the Tongariro Northern Circuit Great Walk, past the Taranaki Falls to the Tama Lakes and return. While crossing fairly gentle terrain, the route is very exposed and not recommended in inclement weather conditions. Carry plenty of water, and be well equipped for a change in weather.

Taranaki Falls 1 hour

From Ngauruhoe Place (a short walk from the DOC visitor centre at Whakapapa), the well-graded and gravelled upper track leads across tussock and shrublands towards Taranaki Falls. An alternative lower route also leads to the falls, passing largely through beech forest. After about an hour the track reaches a footbridge over the Wairere Stream, just above Taranaki Falls. Shortly afterwards take the side track down some stairs to reach a viewpoint of the 20 metre falls tumbling over an old lava flow.

Walker behind Taranaki Falls

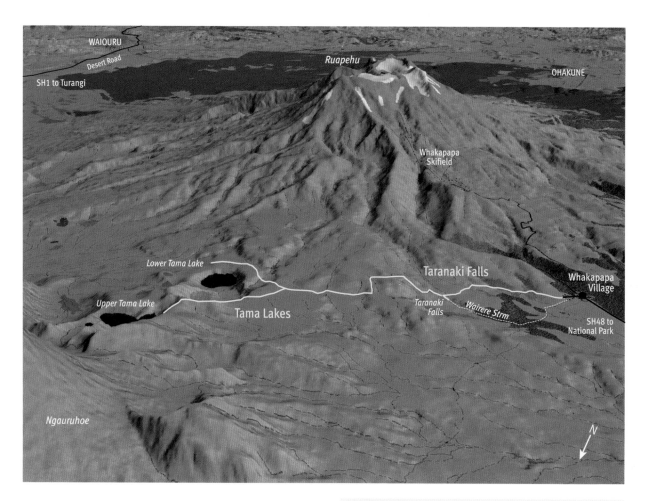

Taranaki Falls to Tama Saddle 60–90 minutes

Back at the main Northern Tongariro Circuit, the poled track heads eastwards across an increasingly barren landscape towards Tama Saddle, the low point between Ngauruhoe and Ruapehu. An hour or so after Taranaki Falls, a signposted track branches off to the north, leading to the Upper Tama Lake, the larger of the two (allow 1.5 hours return). The Lower Tama Lake lies a short distance further along the main track, reached on a short 20 minute return side trip.

Grade Medium
Maps T19 Tongariro, T20 Ruapehu, Tongariro Parkmap
Total Walking Time Lower Tama Lake, 5–6 hours return. Upper Tama Lake, 6–7 hours return.
Access Whakapapa Village is reached on SH 47 and SH 48, from National Park on SH 4. The village has shops, cafes, toilets, carparking and an excellent DOC visitor centre.
Alternative route Taranaki Falls make a worthwhile destination in themselves, and the upper track and lower track in combination form a convenient loop from Whakapapa Village for those who want a shorter (2–2.5 hour) walk.
Information DOC Whakapapa Tel: 07-892-3729

TONGARIRO NATIONAL PARK
LAKE ROTOPOUNAMU

Formed by a landslide some 10,000 years ago, Lake Roto-pounamu (Greenstone Lake) nestles under the protective cone of Mt Pihanga, part of the northern outpost of Tongariro National Park.

The lake's peaceful, bush-surrounded nature, and its jade-coloured waters make the walk around it a popular one. Well-graded and benched, the track will suit walkers of all abilities, and makes an ideal destination for families. The circuit track around the lake can be taken in either direction, but most people chose to walk anti-clockwise, and this certainly reduces the sense of crowding.

Carpark to Lake Rotopounamu 20–30 minutes

From the carpark the track enters podocarp–hardwood forest immediately, and begins a gentle climb over a low bush brow to reach the lake shore. Here a track junction signals a left turn to Ten Minute Beach and a right turn to Five Minute Beach. If you are heading around the lake, take the Five Minute Beach option, which – not surprisingly – is 5 minutes on. During calm days the reflection of Mt Pihanga on the lake surface proves particularly appealing.

Around Lake Rotopounamu 1–1.5 hours

From Five Minute Beach the track heads southwards, keeping more or less close to the shore. At the lake's eastern

Bush-fringed shores of Lake Rotopounamu

extremity, sandy Long Beach makes a perfect picnic or swimming spot (toilets are available). The final section passes around the lake's northern shore to Ten Minute Beach, and back to the start of the circuit. Happily, the walk back to the carpark is mostly downhill.

Grade Easy
Map T19 Tongariro
Total Walking Time 2–2.5 hours round trip
Access From Turangi take SH 41 for 3 km then turn off onto SH 47 for a further 8 km. The large carpark and track start are well signposted on the south side of Te Ponanga Saddle.
Alternative route : Those wanting a shorter walk (40–60 minutes return) can just take the track as far as the lake.
Information DOC Taupo Tel: 07-386-8607

Lake Rotopounamu at dusk

LAKE TAUPO
KAWAKAWA BAY

Peaceful Kawakawa Bay, lying west of Kinloch, offers escape from the throngs of holidaymakers that descend on Taupo during the summer. The bay is reached on a thoroughly enjoyable bush track with good viewpoints over New Zealand's largest lake. While the walk is never taxing, it does involve some climbing. En route are opportunities for swimming and picnicking.

Carpark to Kawakawa Bay 2 hours

There are two ways to start the walk. One option is to go straight from the beach at Kinloch, heading west. In the wrong sort of wind and waves walkers may be pushed into overhanging willows, which can be trying, but generally this is a pleasant route.

Alternatively, a slightly shorter route begins from Nisbet Terrace. This track follows a terrace, soon reaching a footbridge over a stream. Here the track ends temporarily, taking to the beach for 150 metres. Both tracks join where a signpost indicates the track enters the bush again.

The track passes through regenerating forest dominated by five finger, rewarewa, mahoe and rangiora. A gradual

Kawakawa Bay showing emergent rewarewa trees

climb, with one dip down to a stream, eventually leads to a broad peninsula separating Kinloch and Kawakawa bays. Occasional viewpoints offer superb vistas of Lake Taupo and the distant volcanoes of Tongariro National Park. After a total of about 90 minutes walking, the track reaches an excellent viewpoint overlooking Kawakawa Bay. The low pyramid of Mt Pureora and the Hauhungaroa Range dominates the western horizon, and the Otupoto Falls are also visible on the Western Bays. A 20 minute descent leads to Kawakawa Bay, an ideal spot for picnics and swimming.

Grade Easy–Medium

Map T18 Kuratau

Total Walking Time 4–5 hours return

Access From just north of Taupo on SH 1, take Pohipi, Whangamata and Kinloch roads for 24 km to Kinloch (the route is well signposted). The track to Kawakawa Bay begins either from the Kinloch foreshore or from the end of Nisbet Terrace (which runs parallel to the shore).

Alternative route For those wanting a slightly shorter walk (3 hours return), the viewpoint above the bay makes a good turnaround point.

Information DOC Taupo Tel: 07-386-8607

BOUNDARY STREAM SCENIC RESERVE, HAWKE'S BAY
SHINE FALLS

In her wonderful guidebook, Hawke's Bay for the Happy Wanderer, *author Sheila Cunningham described Shine Falls as 'probably the finest falls in Hawke's Bay'. The 58 metre waterfall tumbles over a limestone escarpment in Boundary Stream Scenic Reserve, part of Hawke's Bay's most significant lowland forest remnant. A track runs right through the scenic reserve, with Shine Falls forming the highlight. The eastern approach to the falls makes an easy and delightful bush walk that is appealing to families and walkers of all abilities.*

Since 1996 Boundary Stream has been one of DOC's mainland islands: sites of intensive management where pest numbers are kept low to improve the habitat for native species. North Island brown kiwi, robins, kokako, kaka and karearea (NZ falcon) are amongst the birds thriving in the reserve.

Heay's Access Road to Shine Falls 45–60 minutes

From the carpark, the track crosses a stile and passes over farmland beneath sizeable limestone bluffs and outcrops. Posts mark the route for 20–25 minutes to the reserve boundary. From here an easy, flat track sidles above a gorge in Boundary Stream with limestone cliffs above. In spring, yellow kowhai flowers and the red blooms of the endangered kaka beak add colour to the more sombre greens of the surrounding bush. About 5 minutes before Shine Falls, the track through to Pohokura Road branches off. Continue over a footbridge and past a picnic table to reach a pool at the base of the falls. After heavy rain, expect a drenching from spray.

Grade Easy
Map V20 Esk
Total Walking Time 1.5–2 hours return
Access From Napier drive north on SH 2 for 43 km until just past Lake Tutira. Turn left onto Matahorua Road, follow it for 13 km, then turn right onto Heays Access Road for 7 km to reach the Shine Falls carpark, shelter and picnic area. Allow an hour to drive from Napier.
Alternative route Shine Falls can also be reached from Pohokura Road on the Kamahi Track, in the western part of the Boundary Stream Reserve. Allow a total walking time of 4–5 hours for the through trip to Heays Access Road, best walked in the west–east direction to give an overall descent.
Information DOC Napier Tel: 06-834-3111

Shine Falls, Boundary Stream Scenic Reserve

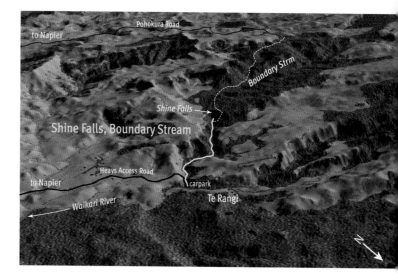

HAWKE'S BAY
OTATARA PA HISTORIC RESERVE

Maori pou pou (carved pole) at Otatara Pa,
Otatara Pa Historic Site

One of the most accessible Maori pa sites in the country, Otatara perches on steep hillsides, its palisaded flanks making an impressive silhouette against the sky. The pa lies on the rural outskirts of Taradale, a suburb of Napier, overlooking the Tutaekuri Valley. DOC rates the pa site as 'one of the largest and most significant traditional archaeological sites in New Zealand'. Occupied for over 500 years by a succession of iwi, the tactically defensive site was chosen for its commanding views over the Heretaunga Plains, and was situated next to a now non-existent lagoon rich in kaimoana (seafood). House sites, terraces, and kumara storage pits are all obvious features at the reserve.

Despite its fascinating past and importance as an historic site, quarrying ate away at its flanks for several decades between 1925 and 1986, and generally the pa site became a neglected and unappreciated place. Fortunately Crown and council purchase of the land in the 1970s paved the way for establishing an historic site. In 1990 the Waiohiki Conservation Corps erected wooden palisades, attracting the interest of locals and giving the site much more physical and cultural prominence. During Maori language week in July 2005 DOC and local iwi opened an excellent new entrance with informative panels on the area's history.

Carpark to Hikurangi Pa 30–40 minutes

From the carpark, a gravelled path leads through the entranceway, where most walkers will want to pause to read the information panels and admire the carved poles. The path climbs gently on an old vehicle track up to the palisaded section of the Otatara Pa, which gives an impression of the original defences. Beyond, the track climbs up farmland, over a couple of stiles, and up to a second pa site known as Hikurangi where kumara pits are prominent. Extensive views extend over Taradale and Napier to the northeast and the Tutaekuri Valley and Heretaunga Plains to the east and south. Descend an easy grass spur back to the carpark.

Grade Easy

Map V21 Napier

Total Walking Time 1–1.5 hours return

Access From Taradale take Gloucester Street (following signs for SH 50) for 1 km, past the Eastern Institute of Technology until just before the road bridge over the Tutaekuri River. The Historic Reserve carpark is well signposted.

Alternative route In the future, it is hoped walkers will be able to link the Otatara tracks with those at the nearby Dolbel Reserve, off Puketapu Road, to create a longer trip. At present this route is not marked and crosses private land between the two reserves.

Information DOC Napier Tel: 06-834-3111

View over Otatara Pa and Tutaekuri Valley, Otatara Pa Historic Site

HAWKE'S BAY
CAPE KIDNAPPERS GANNET RESERVE

Forming the southern boundary of Hawke Bay, Cape Kidnappers earned its European name after an incident on Captain Cook's 1769 journey to New Zealand, when local Maori attempted to kidnap a Tahitian boy on board the Endeavour. *The cape boasts some 7000 pairs of breeding gannets each summer, making it the largest accessible mainland colony of Australasian gannets in the world. The gannets nest in close proximity to each other: a clamouring, smelly spectacle of life, with the elegant adults coming and going to feed their gawky chicks.*

Aside from the gannets, walkers enjoy the cape for its dramatic coastal scenery, and the wide sea views that – on a clear day – extend as far north as Mahia Peninsula. The main Plateau Colony is closed from 30 June until the Wednesday prior to Labour weekend in October. The best time to visit is from early November to late February when chicks have hatched. Those who wish to forego the last section to the Plateau Colony can observe gannets at Black Reef.

Be warned, this is a very popular walk, particularly in December and January – and at low tide walkers will have to share the coastline with tractors, buses and motorbikes. It is necessary to time the walk around low–mid tide to avoid being trapped by an incoming tide on your return.

Australasian gannets, Plateau Colony, Cape Kidnappers Gannet Reserve

Clifton to Black Reef 2–2.5 hours

From the carpark at Clifton, follow the track eastwards, past the campground at Clifton. The beaches generally provide fast travel, especially on the sections of hard-packed sand, but at mid-tide walkers may have to boulder-hop closer to the cliffs. The Cape's intriguing layered cliffs are comprised of sandstone, conglomerate and a mudstone known as papa, laid down over various periods between one and five million years ago. After about 2 hours walking, the first sign of gannets comes at Black Reef, a series of small islets lying just offshore.

Black Reef to Plateau Colony 1–1.5 hours

Beyond Black Reef the coastline sweeps out to Cape Kidnappers with mudstone reefs interspersing sandy beaches. About 25–30 minutes past Black Reef a signposted track heads off through coastal shrubland up to a picnic area with a shelter, water tank, toilets and information panels.

Beyond, a well-formed track climbs stiffly onto a grassy plateau, past a ranger's house, and up another short climb to the Plateau Colony itself.

Grade Medium
Map W21 Kidnappers
Total Walking Time 5–7 hours return
Access From the town of Clive on SH 2, turn off onto Mill Road and follow signposts to Clifton on Parkhill Road, East Road and Clifton Road. At Clifton there is a carpark and information panel. The nearby campground has a shop and toilets.
Alternative route For those who want less walking, commercial operators run trips out to Cape Kidnappers, both along the coast and overland through Summerlee Station.
Information DOC Napier Tel: 06-834-3111

KAWEKA FOREST PARK
KAWEKA J • KAWEKA FLATS

KAWEKA J

Kaweka J (1724 m), one of the highest non-volcanic peaks in the North Island, is the highest peak in Kaweka Forest Park. On a good day it is a grand summit and a popular destination for a day trip, despite involving a 750 metre ascent. Another link in the great axial ranges of the North Island, the Kaweka Range lies north of the Ruahine Range, and south of the Ahimanawa and Huiarau ranges. Its broad summit crest offers views across the bewildering complexity of ridges that stretches across Kaweka Forest Park, through neighbouring Kaimanawa Forest Park and ultimately to the volcanic peaks of Tongariro National Park.

Although 'The J' can be a treacherous place in bad weather, being very exposed to winds from almost every direction, its position in Hawke's Bay means it enjoys more sunshine hours than other mountainous parts of the country. For those with alpine skills and an ice axe, it makes a worthy winter summit. Dominie Biv, a cute two-bunker, provides some shelter en route and a place to fill the water bottle. It makes a good destination for those who don't wish to push on to the summit.

Makahu Saddle to Dominie Biv (2 bunks) 1.5–2 hours

From Makahu Saddle carpark a signposted track leads past Makahu Saddle Hut (one of the earliest Forest Service huts built in the area), the last place to get water before the biv. Past the hut a short section of flat travel leads to a zigzag ascent up Trials Spur. In recent years DOC have cut the extensive lodgepole pine forests that once smothered this spur and those around it. Soon after reaching the first of the subalpine herbfields, Trials Spur joins the main Makahu Spur. Fifteen minutes from here lies Dominie Biv, perched on a flat shoulder with commanding views of North Kaweka.

Dominie to Kaweka J 1–1.5 hours

Beyond Dominie Biv, follow the poled and defined route upwards. After sidling around a few rocky outcrops, the gradient eases until it finally flattens out on the wide range crest. Here, the Kaweka J route intercepts a poled route that goes north–south along the main range. Head south on this route across gentle terrain to the summit of Kaweka J, which is marked by an old wooden trig and a large memorial cairn nearby.

Grade Medium–Hard
Maps U20 Kaweka, Kaweka Parkmap.
Total Walking Time 4–6 hours return
Access From Napier drive 60 km to Puketitiri. Shortly beyond Puketitiri, take a left fork into Whittle Road, follow it for 5 km, then turn right onto Kaweka Road. Follow this past Littles Clearing to the Makahu Saddle carpark, where there are toilets, and an information panel. Chains may be necessary in winter. In total, allow for a good 90 minute drive from Napier.
Alternative route On the descent, walkers can opt to descend the full length of Makahu Spur instead of using Trials Spur. Both routes join again near the carpark.
Information DOC Napier Tel: 06-834-3111

KAWEKA FLATS

Kaweka Flats provides a gentler alternative to an ascent of Kaweka J, and also offers walkers an option when the weather is too unforgiving for the tops. Although the walk mainly traverses an undulating track through beech forest, there are sufficient viewpoints en route to satisfy the eye. During the late 1800s and early 1900s, the open clearing at Kaweka Flats was used as a holding area for sheep during musters. Those with suitable navigational nous can find their way to the nearby historic Iron Whare, a totara slab hut probably built during the 1870s. It has the distinction of being the oldest hut in the Hawke's Bay Conservancy, and one of the oldest back-country huts in the country. Kaweka Flats Biv is a classic 'dog box' biv dating from the New Zealand Forest Service deer culling era of the 1950s; a piece of history in its own right.

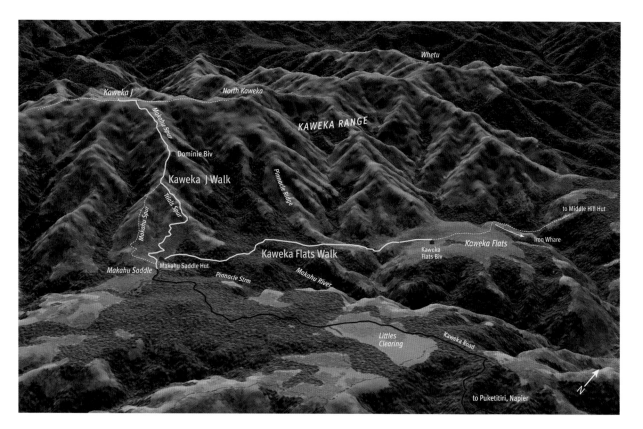

Makahu Saddle to Kaweka Flats Biv (2 bunks) 1.5–2 hours

From Makahu Saddle carpark a signposted track leads past Makahu Saddle Hut (one of the earliest Forest Service huts built in the area) then beyond to cross Pinnacle Stream. From here the track contours around forested slopes to a crossing of the Makahu River. More undulating travel and three more stream crossings lead to the clearing at Kaweka Flats. On a good day there are views up the craggy profile of Pinnacle Ridge and to North Kaweka.

Kaweka Flats Biv to Iron Whare 30–40 minutes each way

Map U20 shows the location of the Iron Whare accurately, but does not indicate the route to the historic hut. From Kaweka Flats head north along the track towards Middle Hill Hut. Just before the track begins a descent into a branch of the Makahu River, an indistinct, unmarked trail heads east along a bush ridge to the Iron Whare. The route is suitable only for walkers competent with a compass and map.

Grade Medium

Maps U20 Kaweka, Kaweka Parkmap.

Total Walking Time 4–6 hours return

Access From Napier drive 60 km to Puketitiri. Shortly beyond Puketitiri, take a left fork into Whittle Road, follow it for 5 km, then turn right onto Kaweka Road. Follow this past Littles Clearing to the Makahu Saddle carpark, where there are toilets, and an information panel. Chains may be necessary in winter. In total, allow for a good 90 minute drive from Napier.

Information DOC Napier Tel: 06-834-3111

RUAHINE FOREST PARK
SUNRISE HUT

The Ruahine Range, separating Hawke's Bay from the Mana-watu and Rangitikei, is part of the North Island's great axial range that extends for several hundred kilometres between Wellington and East Cape. Beech forest dominates the eastern flanks of the Ruahine Range, which rises to tops dominated by crags, tussock grasslands and scree slopes.

The easiest access onto the tops is on the Sunrise Track, a high-quality, well-graded track that climbs up a forested spur to Sunrise Hut. The recently enlarged hut occupies a charming subalpine basin overlooking the farmland and distant coast-line of Hawke's Bay. Although involving a reasonable climb, Sunrise Hut is a good destination for families with school-age children. Families with younger children can enjoy the shorter loop around the Swamp Track past Triplex Hut and back to the carpark.

North Block Road Carpark to Sunrise Hut (20 bunks, gas heater, gas cookers, $10/night) 2.5–3 hours

From the carpark, the Sunrise Track leads across farmland for a short distance to a fence at the edge of the bush. Cross a stile here to reach the Swamp Track, which passes through a flat section of podocarp–beech forest.

En route, signposts indicate two side tracks to Triplex Hut (12 bunks, wood stove, $5/night), one halfway along the Swamp Track, and another where the Sunrise Track begins. The track climbs immediately, zigzagging lazily up the forested ridge. The bushline is reached after 2–3 hours of moderate ascent. Sunrise Hut is nearby, set amongst subalpine plants, a small tarn and a patch of stunted forest in Buttercup Hollow.

In favourable weather a stroll along to Armstrong Saddle will yield views of the distant volcanoes of Ruapehu and Ngauruhoe. From the hut this poled route skirts the edge of some imposing erosion scars before a short climb to the saddle (1369 m). The saddle is named after pioneer aviator Hamish Armstrong, who crashed here in 1935 and, though surviving the impact, died in his attempt to get help.

Opposite *Sunrise Hut in Buttercup Hollow, Armstrong Saddle*

Grade Medium
Maps U22 Ongaonga, Ruahine Parkmap
Total Walking Time 5–7 hours return
Access From SH 50, just north of Ongaonga, turn left onto Wakarara Road. Follow this to Wakarara, where you turn left onto North Block Road. The carpark lies near the farm–bush boundary.
Alternative route Halfway back down the Sunrise track, a trail branches off south to Waipawa Forks Hut and the Waipawa River, providing an alternative route back to your vehicle. This route involves river crossings and would be unwise to attempt after heavy rain.
Information DOC Napier Tel: 06-834-3111

TARARUA FOREST PARK
MT HOLDSWORTH • ATIWHAKATU VALLEY

MT HOLDSWORTH

With commanding views over the Wairarapa, the large and modern Powell Hut is the most popular hut in Tararua Forest Park, and makes a convenient place from which to tackle nearby Mt Holdsworth (1470 m). Holdsworth has attracted walkers for over a century, with the first hut in the area – Mountain House – built in 1907. One Masterton tramper, Eric McIntosh, has climbed the peak over 400 times.

While the track is well-marked and graded, this is still a strenuous walk involving a solid 1200 metre ascent, and the final section above the hut to Mt Holdsworth is exposed and unmarked. During winter, trampers will require an ice axe and possibly crampons too.

Mt Holdsworth Road to Powell Hut (32 bunks, gas cookers, gas heater) 3–4 hours

From the carpark a gravelled track leads up the valley past Holdsworth Lodge (sign the intentions book here) to a footbridge over the Atiwhakatu Stream. After another 10 minutes upvalley, the track forks: head left up the well-benched and gravelled Gentle Annie Track, which climbs steadily through mixed beech–hardwood–podocarp forest. A short side track to Rocky Lookout offers views. More undulating ridge travel ensues, past the Totara Flats track that branches off to the left. Near Pig Flat the three-sided Mountain House Shelter offers a place for eating provisions or a pause. Above Mountain House, the track steepens, emerging above the bushline and scrambling up a couple of rocky sections before reaching Powell Hut.

Powell Hut to Mt Holdsworth 1 hour

Above Powell Hut a well-worn (but not poled) route leads up tussock slopes to Mt Holdsworth, marked by a trig station. On a good day, there are views eastwards over the Wairarapa; westwards into the rugged Waiohine Valley; and along the tawny tops of the Tararua Range stretching northwards towards Jumbo, Angle Knob and McGregor.

Grade Hard
Maps S26 Carterton, Tararua Recreation map
Total Walking Time 7–8 hours return
Access From SH 2, just south of Masterton, turn off onto Norfolk Road. This eventually becomes Mt Holdsworth Road. At the road end is a large carpark, camping area, toilets and Holdsworth Lodge (available for overnight stays). The caretaker takes lodge bookings on Tel: 06-377-0022
Alternative route From Mt Holdsworth very fit and experienced trampers can tackle the route across the tops to Jumbo Hut and down into the Atiwhakatu Valley (see Atiwhakatu Valley walk). A track down east Holdsworth ridge to the Atiwhakatu is another possibility. A less exposed circuit is the track into the Atiwhakatu Valley from Mountain House.
Information DOC Masterton Tel: 06-377-0700

ATIWHAKATU VALLEY

The delightful, forested Atiwhakatu Valley is an attractive destination for walkers of all abilities. Draining the eastern side of the Tararua Range in the vicinity of Mt Holdsworth, Atiwhakatu Stream is one of the more scenic and accessible of those in Tararua Forest Park. An all-weather route, the walk also makes a good alternative to the Mt Holdsworth tramp when conditions on the tops look unpleasant.

Mt Holdsworth Road to Atiwhakatu Hut (8 bunks, open fire) 3 hours

From the carpark follow a gravelled track up the valley, stopping at Holdsworth Lodge to sign the intentions book. Shortly beyond, the track crosses the Atiwhakatu Stream on a footbridge. Soon afterwards the track reaches a signposted junction. Avoid the one leading uphill (this is the Gentle Annie Track to Mt Holdsworth) and stay on the well-benched and gravelled Atiwhakatu Valley track.

After another 10 minutes the track reaches the substantial

Donnelly Flat, where there are camping spots and picnic tables. From the end of the flats, the track sidles above a gorge in the Atiwhakatu Stream, with footbridges crossing a couple of side streams en route. A large arched bridge spans the sizeable Holdsworth Creek. Beyond, the track levels out somewhat for the final section to Atiwhakatu Hut, a classic New Zealand Forest Service hut dating from the deer culling era of the 1960s.

Grade Easy–Medium

Maps S26 Carterton, Tararua Recreation map

Total Walking Time 5–6 hours return

Access From SH 2, just south of Masterton, turn off onto Norfolk Road. This eventually becomes Mt Holdsworth Road. At the road end is a large carpark, camping area, toilets and Holdsworth Lodge (available for overnight stays). The caretaker takes lodge bookings on Tel: 06-377-0022

Alternative route Those wanting a shorter walk can turn back at any number of places; Donnelly Flat or Holdsworth Stream being obvious landmarks. Trampers who enjoy getting wet might like to follow the river downstream from Atiwhakatu Hut: this involves multiple river crossings and some swims through deep pools in the gorge. If in doubt about your ability or rising river levels, exit the gorge at Holdsworth Stream and scramble back up to the track.

Information DOC Masterton Tel: 06-377-0700

WAIRARAPA
CASTLEPOINT SCENIC RESERVE

Of all the scenic coastlines of the Wairarapa, Castlepoint is undoubtedly the most fascinating. Indeed, there is no other coastal landform in New Zealand remotely like it. The Castlepoint lighthouse perches atop an old limestone reef, raised out of the sea like an upturned ship's hull. Southwards, the reef forms a low protective barrier against the surf, almost encircling the aptly named Deliverance Cove, through which many a fishing boat has retreated to safety from heavy seas. And above it all rises the monolithic Castle Rock, a coastal knoll flanked by cliffs and offering expansive views.

The walk to the Castlepoint lighthouse suits walkers and families of all abilities, although parents have to watch their children closely around cliff edges. Nearby Castle Rock entails a 162 metre ascent, requiring a modest level of fitness. Fishing boats, launched on large, specially designed trailers with very long towbars, form another interesting aspect of the area.

Adjacent to the scenic reserve is the small Castlepoint Beach community. A campground and shop service visitors and locals alike.

Carpark to Castlepoint Lighthouse 20–30 minutes return

From the carpark cross the sandy isthmus to a bridge that straddles the channel out of Deliverance Cove. A well-graded path leads up a gentle slope to the prominent lighthouse, built in 1913. Above the lighthouse a recently developed set of wooden stairs leads to a viewing platform with a fine vista of the coastline north and south. Stairs continue to loop around the headland amongst coastal vegetation back to the lighthouse. Keep an observant eye out for shellfish fossils.

Carpark to Deliverance Cove and Castle Rock Summit 1–1.5 hours return

Walk around the sandy shore of Deliverance Cove to where an obvious but unmarked trail leads into the dunes at the base of Castle Rock. From here the trail zigzags solidly uphill over grassy slopes, reaching a small saddle. From here a side trail leads down to Christmas Cove, a pleasant sandy bay.

The main trail zigzags ever upwards, cresting the eastern edge of Castle Rock just before the summit. In strong winds watch your step, and stay away from the edge – a fall from here would be fatal.

Grade Easy
Map U26 Castle Point
Total Walking Time 2 hours return, combining both walks
Access From the northern outskirts of Masterton, turn right onto Te Ore Ore Road, following signposts to Castlepoint. The road becomes the Masterton–Castlepoint Road which ends at the beach. Allow an hour for the 50 km drive from Masterton.
Alternative route From the saddle below Castle Rock a high level track leads around farmland and through a patch of pine trees back to the carpark.
Information DOC Masterton Tel: 06-377-0700

Above Sunrise on cliffs at Castlepoint. **Opposite** A family descends towards Castlepoint lighthouse

WAIRARAPA
PUTANGIRUA PINNACLES SCENIC RESERVE

Perhaps the most bizarre landform in the Wairarapa, and certainly the most distinctive, the Putangirua Pinnacles look like the 'badlands' formations of some North American prairie landscapes. The pinnacles – or hoodoos – consist of partially cemented greywacke gravels that have survived the eroding forces of the Putangirua Stream. Many pillars feature an erosion-resistant cap, and some are thought to be around 1000 years old.

Water and wind continue to work change on this very dynamic landscape, and walkers need to be aware of the area's unstable nature; watch for falling rocks, especially after heavy rain.

The Putangirua Pinnacles lie in a scenic reserve of the same name, bordering Aorangi Forest Park near Palliser Bay. At the carpark is a pleasant camping and picnic area. Walkers and families of all abilities will be able to reach the pinnacles, except when heavy rain makes the stream unfordable. The Loop Track involves a 200 metre climb for which walkers will need a modest level of fitness.

Carpark to Pinnacles 20–30 minutes

From the carpark head up the gravelly riverbed of the Putangirua Stream, which at this point has little to suggest the wonders that lie upstream. There is normally a worn set of footprints, except after floods. Pass the Bush Walk Track entrance, and then after 15–20 minutes pass the Loop Track entrance. Further up, the stream narrows, entering the pinnacles themselves. Many hours could be spent exploring various gullies. Head back to the Loop Track entrance passed on the way in.

Pinnacles to Carpark via Loop and Bush Walk Tracks 1–1.5 hours

The Loop Track climbs steeply through forest to intercept the Bush Walk Track on the main ridge. There is a good vantage point overlooking the pinnacles en route. Take the Bush Walk Track in the downhill direction, and follow it until it emerges just upstream of the camping area and carpark.

Grade Easy
Maps S28 Palliser
Total Walking Time 1.5–2 hours return
Access From Featherston turn off SH 2 onto SH 63 and drive to Martinborough. The Martinborough–Pirinoa Road eventually becomes Whangaimoana and Whatarangi roads. Thirteen kilometres past the Lake Ferry turnoff, just past where the road first hugs the coastline, is Te Kopi. After a further 500 metres, a signposted road branches off to the camping area and carpark at Putangirua Pinnacles Scenic Reserve. Allow an hour to drive from Martinborough.
Alternative route From the lookout, keen walkers might like to continue up to a bulldozed track which leads down to Te Kopi. Allow an extra 2 hours.
Information DOC Masterton Tel: 06-377-0700

EGMONT NATIONAL PARK
DAWSON FALLS & WILKIES POOLS • MANGOREI TRACK & POUAKAI RANGE

DAWSON FALLS AND WILKIES POOLS

Egmont may be New Zealand's second-smallest national park at 33,500 hectares, but it boasts myriad walks and tramps to suit people of all abilities. The walk described here carves a loop through Egmont's characteristic 'goblin forest', past Wilkies Pools and Dawson Falls, two of the scenic highlights in this southeastern sector of the park. The 18 metre Dawson Falls plunge over an escarpment created by a lava flow some 1800 years ago. The smaller cascades of Wilkies Pools also flow over lava, but from a much older eruption that occurred some 20,000 years ago – enough time for water to sculpt the raw rock into channels and flutings of some beauty.

There is a veritable spiderweb of trails in the area, so take a map and pay close attention to all signposts. The walk begins and ends at the Dawson Falls Visitor Centre, accessible on a narrow road that probes into the park from near the south Taranaki township of Eltham. It is suitable for walkers of moderate experience and families with school-age children.

Dawson Falls Visitor Centre to Wilkies Pools
30–40 minutes

From Dawson Falls take the track past the Ben Shaw Shelter. This follows a ridge beside Kapuni Stream, climbing a series of stairs on the well-formed Wilkies Pool Loop Track (red arrows). The so-called 'goblin forest' of Egmont National Park is a mixture of Hall's totara, kamahi and other broadleaf tree species that – due to altitude and heavy rainfall – often become both gnarled and festooned with moss. After 5 minutes or so the Kamahi Dell Loop Track branches off to the left. Carry on uphill, past another junction, following the sign that indicates Wilkies Pools.

Soon after crossing the open riverbed of the Kapuni Stream, the track reaches another junction at Wilkies Pools. A one-way track leads over rocks on the true left of the series of pools (watch your footing after rain, and be mindful of children here). It ends at an open riverbed above the last

Wilkies Pools, Egmont National Park

Mt Taranaki / Egmont

Stony River

Dover Rd

Pouakai

Dover Track

The Dome

Pouakai Track

Ahukawakawa
Swamp

Pouakai Hut

Mangorei Track

Dawson Falls / Wilkies Pools

Fanthams
Peak Track

Wilkies Pools

Dawson Falls

Dawson
Falls

North Egmont

Mangorei Strm

East Egmont

to New Plymouth

of the pools. Wilkies Pools are named after the Wilkie brothers who were local farmers and climbers.

Wilkies Pools to Dawson Falls via Ridge Loop Track 60–80 minutes

Back at the last track junction, continue on the Wilkies Pools Loop Track, which sidles around lush forest, through avenues of foxgloves, past one miniature waterfall and crosses some boardwalks and footbridges. At another track junction divert off the Wilkies Pools Loop Track to the Ridge Track. This climbs a series of steps onto a narrow ridge where stunted, moss-encrusted Hall's totara dominates. The track is generally good travel but can be a bit muddy and rutted in a couple of places. The Ridge Track joins the Kapuni Loop Track (pink arrows) after crossing a footbridge over the Kapuni Stream at a thin but thunderous gorge.

Some 20–25 minutes along the Kapuni Loop Track a short side track leads to the base of Dawson Falls down a series of concrete steps.

Dawson Falls to Visitor Centre via Kapuni Loop Track 30–40 minutes

Although it is possible to go directly back to the visitor centre using a short link track to the road, a more pleasant option is to continue on the Kapuni Loop Track, which arcs back to the carpark, past Konini Lodge. A short distance back down the road, another worthwhile diversion is the 2 minute track to the Dawson Falls Power Station, a small hydro scheme installed in 1935 and the longest continuously running one in New Zealand.

Grade Easy–Medium

Maps P20 Egmont, Egmont National Park Map

Total Walking Time 2–3 hours return

Access From the south Taranaki town of Eltham, take Eltham Road west to Kaponga for 12 km, then head north on Manaia Road, which ends after another 14 km at a carpark beside the Dawson Falls Visitor Centre, which has plenty of good information and displays. Toilets and a shelter are nearby.

Alternative route Keen walkers might like to extend their tramp to include the Waingongoro Hut and gorge.

Information DOC Stratford Tel: 06-765-5144, Email: dawsonfallsvc@doc.govt.nz

MANGOREI TRACK AND POUAKAI RANGE

The undulating tops of the Pouakai Range are essentially the eroded stumps of an old volcano that, some 250,000 years ago, may have had a similar height and shape to Mt Taranaki. Lying in the north of Egmont National Park, the Pouakai Range offers arguably the best vantage point of Mt Taranaki, which lies separated from the range by the large Ahukawakawa Swamp.

The quickest route to the Pouakai Range is the Mangorei Track, accessible from just south of New Plymouth. This historic trail to the mountain, one that predates the formation of the national park in 1900, ascends through an altitudinal sequence of forest to reach Pouakai Hut, situated near the crest of the range just above the bushline.

While the sometimes steep 700 metre ascent and often-times muddy track will deter some walkers, those of moderate fitness and experience will appreciate this outstanding place from which to admire New Zealand's second highest volcano.

Mangorei Track to Pouakai Hut (16 bunks, wood stove, $10/night) 2.5–3 hours

From the carpark the track passes through a brief section of farmland before entering the national park boundary. Climbing gradually, the track ascends slopes through podocarp–hardwood forest before gaining a ridge. A series of steps ensures you gain height quickly. The final section sidles up the flanks of a gully in the head of Mangorei Stream. Here the vegetation becomes increasingly stunted, with mountain cedar forming sometimes fantastical shapes. Pouakai Hut lies just above the bushline, facing north to look over the Taranaki Bight and New Plymouth. Beyond the hut, a further 5 minute walk leads to the crest of the Pouakai Range. Take a worthwhile amble east over boardwalks for 15 minutes or so to a saddle where – on a calm day – tarns reflect the symmetrical volcano to fine effect. During summer, eyebrights and foxgloves are abundant on these tops. Below is Ahukawakawa Swamp, formed when debris flows blocked the Stony River behind a lava plug known as the Dome.

Grade Medium

Maps P20 Egmont, Egmont Parkmap

Total Walking Time 5–6 hours return

Access From New Plymouth, take SH 3 towards Inglewood for about 5 km, before turning off onto Mangorei Road. Follow this for about 14 km before it ends at a carpark and the track start.

Alternative route Fit and experienced trampers can tackle the through route from Pouakai Hut which crosses the Pouakai Range to Dover Road using the Dover Track. (Grade: Hard, allow 6–8 hours for the through trip.)

Information DOC New Plymouth Tel: 06-759-0350

Mt Taranaki from the Pouakai Range

TARANAKI
WHITECLIFFS WALKWAY

The Whitecliffs Walkway forges a passage across farmland and through bush, high above sheer sandstone cliffs that are constantly pummelled by the Tasman Sea.

It is not often that heavy industry actually improves walking opportunities, but in the case of the Whitecliffs Walkway this is undeniably true. Laying the underground Kapuni to Auckland gas pipe during the late 1960s meant cutting through the dense forests of north Taranaki, and a considerable part of the walkway now follows this line.

The walkway connects the tiny Taranaki settlements of Pukearuhe and Tongaporutu, both accessible off SH 3, north of New Plymouth. Instead of following the full walkway, a much more appealing route (and a round trip) is to follow the walkway from Pukearuhe to the Te Horo Stock Tunnel, then return to Pukearuhe along the spectacular coastline.

While undoubtedly one of the most spectacular coastlines in the North Island, walkers should note that this coastal section can be dangerous in the wrong conditions. Never tackle this section at anything other than within 2 hours either side of low tide. After heavy rain be aware that the Waipingau Stream may be unfordable, and the rocks falling from the cliffs may be potentially hazardous. Between 1 July and 30 September the walkway is closed for lambing.

Pukearuhe to Waipingau Stream via Walkway
1.5 hours

From Pukearuhe follow the road past a farmhouse and beyond onto a muddy farm track. For the first hour or so the walkway crosses private farmland climbing gradually until a final steepish push to the ridge crest (241 m) west of Mt Davidson. Here, the track enters the Whitecliffs Conservation Area. It follows the route of the underground pipeline along the ridge through regenerating forest, with occasional views, before descending to the Waipingau Stream on a long series of wooden steps. The main walkway continues northwards across a footbridge over the Waipingau Stream.

Opposite and right *Sandstone cliffs on the coastal section of Whitecliffs Walkway*

Waipingau Stream to Pukearuhe via coast
1.5 hours

This track allows a shortcut through to the coast, avoiding the northern section of the walkway, and the Te Horo Stock Tunnel. Instead of following the walkway over the footbridge, follow the true left of the Waipingau Stream for 20 minutes along a muddy track to the coast, passing a grassy picnic area surrounded by nikau-studded forest en route (a toilet is available). Head south along the rocky coastline, with views of the dramatic cliffs above. Sea arches, wave-sorted boulders, rock towers and black sand make this an intriguing coastline. Note that this section must only be attempted within 2 hours either side of low tide.

Waipingau Stream to Te Horo Stock Tunnel via
Walkway 2 hours

Across the footbridge over the Waipingau Stream, the main walkway begins a steady ascent through lush coastal forest on the Parininihi ridge to the high point of the walkway at 252 metres. Further along the ridge crest a tramping track to Mt Messenger branches off at a signposted junction.

Follow the walkway northwards. Soon it begins a descent down a series of wooden steps that ends at farmland in a gully. A track junction indicates two choices: continue north along the walkway to Tongaporutu, or head south along the coastline to Pukearuhe through the Te Horo Stock Tunnel.

Te Horo Stock Tunnel to Pukearuhe via Coast 3.5 hours

Note that this section must be tackled within the 2 hours either side of low tide. A track leads to the Te Horo Stock Tunnel, built in the 1870s by the military to enable stock to be driven along the coast. The tunnel slopes sharply downwards towards the coast, with slippery footing in places. It ends with rusty iron steps leading onto the black sand. Southward, walk beneath the forbidding Whitecliffs, which tower some 200 metres overhead. Offshore lies the Parininihi Marine Reserve. The ford of Waipingau Stream marks the halfway point back to Pukearuhe.

Waikokora Stream to Tongaporutu 1.5 hours

The last section of the walkway largely follows the Clifton Road across farmland to end at Tongaporutu.

Grade Medium–Hard
Maps Q18 Tongaporutu
Total Walking Time Full walkway, 5–6 hours each way; Pukearuhe–Waipingau Stream Loop, 3 hours round trip; Pukearuhe – Walkway – Te Horo – Coastline loop, 6–7 hours round trip.
Access From Mimi, on SH 3 north of New Plymouth, turn off onto Pukearuhe Road and follow it for 11 km to Pukearuhe. There is only room for parking a couple of cars beside a DOC information panel.
Information DOC New Plymouth Tel: 06-759-0350

WHANGANUI NATIONAL PARK
BRIDGE TO NOWHERE

The Bridge to Nowhere might just be the most famous bridge in the country after the Auckland Harbour Bridge. The bridge, which spans the Mangapurua Stream, a major tributary of the Whanganui River, serves as a symbol of failed farms and hardship. In 1917, the government opened the forested valley to soldiers returning from World War I. Swapping trench spades for bush axes, the soldiers undertook the back-breaking task of clearing dense bush to make farmland in what was an ultimately futile exercise. While a swingbridge across the Mangapurua initially served as access into the valley from the Whanganui River, the government eventually built the current vehicle bridge in 1935–36. However the difficult conditions, and a devastating 1942 flood (which washed out large parts of the Mangapurua Valley road), saw most families abandon their farms during World War II. The significant concrete structure now stands incongruously in dense bush dominated by lush tree ferns that have long since reclaimed the approaches on either side.

Access to the bridge is possible on a 2 day tramp from Whakahoro Hut, but walkers need to approach by jet boat. From Pipiriki it is an exhilarating ride up the sinuous coils of the Whanganui River to the Mangapurua Landing, where the walk begins. Suitable for walkers of most abilities, the track would make a great day's outing for family groups.

Mangapurua Landing to Bridge to Nowhere
40–60 minutes one way

After disembarking the jet boat, the track begins a sidle above the Whanganui River, before turning up the Mangapurua Valley. More sidling ensues, crossing a footbridge before rounding a headland and sidling onto a flattish bush terrace. The Mangapurua narrows through a gorge, with the track sidling high above, shortly before reaching the historic bridge.

Grade Easy
Maps P20 Egmont, Whanganui Parkmap
Total Walking Time 1.5–2 hours return
Access Pipiriki lies about 1.5–2 hours drive (79 km) from Wanganui on the winding but historically interesting Whanganui River Road. Alternatively access is from Raetihi, off SH 4. At Pipiriki a number of commercial jet boat operators are available; try contacting the Wanganui i-Site searching 'Bridge to Nowhere' or 'Whanganui River' on the internet.
Alternative route Those wanting a longer walk can continue on the track up the Mangapurua Valley for as long as energy and interest allows.
Information DOC Wanganui Tel: 06-348-8475, Wanganui i-Site Tel: 06 349-0508

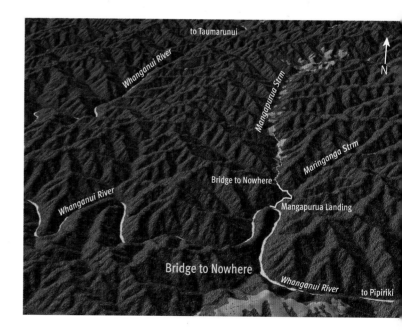

WANGANUI
BUSHY PARK

Bushy Park, a 98 hectare podocarp–hardwood reserve north-west of Wanganui, is an important and rare example of virgin lowland forest that has never been milled. The Moore family, who farmed in the area for several generations, preserved the bush, and in 1962 Frank Moore donated it to Royal Forest & Bird Protection Society. The fine old Edwardian homestead is available for overnight stays or functions.

Walkers are likely to hear the heavy flurry of kereru wings and the chiming of tui, two very common birds in the park. Other birds include tomtits, fantails, grey warblers, falcons and North Island robins (reintroduced in 2001). Through the Bushy Park Trust, Forest & Bird and volunteers have controlled pests in the reserve since 1994, and in 2005 encircled the entire reserve with a predator-proof fence. Vulnerable birds like kokako, kiwi, and tieke are to be reintroduced.

Although none of the walks here are individually longer than an hour, walkers could happily spend half a day or more wandering around this tranquil forest. An enormous Northern rata – probably the largest in the country – forms another highlight. The homestead, with its magnificent stained-glass entranceway and elegant rooms, is also worth wandering around.

Bushy Park makes an ideal location to take children on their first bush walk.

Suggested loop around the Ratanui, Twin Ponga, Homestead, Boundary, Kapiti and Kauri tracks
1.5–2 hours

The Ratanui Track begins behind the homestead, where there are toilets and a small information centre. Follow it for 5 minutes until the Twin Ponga Track branches off. The highlight of this track is a double-stemmed silver fern, growing amongst verdant forest featuring nikau palms. After a 10–15 minute loop, the Twin Ponga Track rejoins the Ratanui Track. A further 10 minutes leads to Ratanui, a voluminous Northern rata with an impressive 12 metre

Ratanui, thought to be the largest Northern rata in New Zealand

girth, towering 48 metres above the ground. From the rata, take the Homestead Track, a narrower, less-formed track that strikes towards the park boundary, passing through dense stands of tawa en route. At the boundary is a picnic table. Head south along the fenceline, which provides a striking contrast between the forest on the inside and the farmland beyond. Shrubby mahoe and kawakawa dominate the forest edge. After a 25–30 minute walk, the track crosses a stile, into an area of gum forest, before striking into the native forest once again on the Kapiti Track. This ends on the access road after 15 minutes, but the Kauri Track soon branches off, leading back to the homestead past a small grove of kauri planted in the 1940s or '50s.

Grade Easy
Map R22 Wanganui
Total Walking Time 1.5–2 hours return
Access Bushy Park is 24 km from Wanganui. At Kai Iwi turn off SH 3 onto Rangitatau East Road at a well signposted junction. The entrance branches off to the left after 8 km. Access to the reserve is through two electric gates operated by push-buttons.
Alternative route Walkers may like to add the 30 minute Wetlands Walk to their itinerary. It begins and ends near the Kauri track in the Homestead grounds.
Information Bushy Park Homestead Tel: 06-342-9879, www: bushyparkhomestead.co.nz
Entry costs $6 per adult; children 15 or under are free.

WELLINGTON
BUTTERFLY CREEK, EAST HARBOUR REGIONAL PARK •
ORONGORONGO TRACK, RIMUTAKA FOREST PARK

BUTTERFLY CREEK, EAST HARBOUR REGIONAL PARK

Wellingtonians are fortunate to have on their back door such an accessible yet remote-feeling spot as Butterfly Creek. Butterfly Creek, a small stream running seawards from the hills behind the suburb of Eastbourne, lies in one of several regional parks in Wellington. Four different tracks lead to a delightfully secluded picnic area, set in a partial clearing amongst a copse of beech trees. Between the 1930s and 1950s a small kiosk, serving tea and scones, operated in this unlikely location.

It is a wonderful destination for families and walkers of all abilities, and the four tracks offer the possibility of several through or round trips. The one described below makes an excellent through trip. Walkers may see butterflies in the area, but the name probably originated from a lepidopteran-shaped patch of vegetation in the valley, which has since become unrecognisable.

Kowhai Track to Butterfly Creek picnic area
45–60 minutes

This track provides the quickest access to Butterfly Creek, with the least amount of climbing. From Kowhai Road, the well-benched, hard-surfaced track begins a climb, zigzagging through regenerating forest, where views of Matiu/Somes Island unfold. After 25–30 minutes the Bus Barn Track branches off. From here the track descends through mature beech forest to join the MacKenzie Track after another 10 minutes. Head right (downstream) along a shady valley dominated by rimu, nikau and silver ferns. After 15–20 minutes the track crosses a footbridge over Gollans Stream to reach the Butterfly Creek picnic area. There is a composting toilet nearby.

Matiu/Somes Island from the lookout on Mackenzie Road Track

Butterfly Creek to MacKenzie Road 1.5–2 hours

Head back to the Kowhai Track junction, but here continue northwards along the well-benched MacKenzie Track. This leads up Butterfly Creek, crossing several footbridges, climbing gradually through lush forest. Past the last footbridge, the track zigzags steadily to reach an excellent lookout at the junction of the MacKenzie Road Track and Muritai Park Track junction. From the bench seat enjoy great views of Wellington Harbour and its islands. The MacKenzie Road Track descends steadily through manuka and gorse (the result of past fires) to a set of stairs above MacKenzie Road.

Grade Easy
Maps R27, R28 Wellington
Total Walking Time 2.5–3 hours
Access Access is from Kowhai Road, in the Wellington suburb of Eastbourne. Buses service the area.
Information Wellington Regional Council Tel: 04-384-5708, www.gw.govt.nz

ORONGORONGO TRACK, RIMUTAKA FOREST PARK

The Rimutaka Range is where the North Island's mountainous spine, which begins at East Cape and stretches for some 500 kilometres, finally bows into the sea. Draining the range, and flowing out to Cook Strait, is the Orongorongo River, a river much loved by Wellington walkers. Many keen trampers have experienced their first overnight tramp using one of the 70-odd private huts that lie hidden away in the valley's forests. Access to the valley is on one of the country's most popular walks, the Orongorongo Track. Perhaps the track's most appealing quality is the diversity of forest types through which it weaves.

This is an ideal walk for walkers of all abilities and family groups wanting their first taste of the back country. Five DOC-managed huts in the valley are available for booking for those who would like to extend their walk to an overnight trip.

Catchpool to Turere Bridge 1.5–2 hours

From the carpark the track climbs past an area of recently milled pine forest to soon enter native forest. A gentle descent leads to the valley floor of the Catchpool Stream, where nikau palms and kiekie vines give the place an unexpected lushness. Information panels erected by the Rimutaka Forest Park Trust explains some of the track's natural history. In 2006 the Trust reintroduced North Island brown kiwi into the neighbouring Turere Valley, the first time the birds have had a presence in the Rimutaka Range for some 300 years.

Soon the track reaches an area of open red beech trees. Later, pockets of rimu and miro dominate over the more ubiquitous kamahi. Footbridges span all but the most insignificant side creeks, and gradually the track crests an almost imperceptible rise. Beyond, the track descends, gently at first, but then more noticeably, to end at an arched bridge over the Turere Stream, near its confluence with the gravelly expanse of the Orongorongo River. Kids will enjoy messing around with stones in the pool below the bridge, and the riverbed makes a fine place for a picnic. Toilets are situated just upvalley.

Grade Easy
Map R27/28 Wellington
Total Walking Time 3–4 hours return
Access From Wellington, drive to Wainuiomata, then head south along the Coast Road. After about 10 km a signpost indicates the turnoff to the Catchpool valley. There are toilets and information panels at the Catchpool carpark, and several camping areas nearby.
Huts Jans, Shamrock, Raukawa, Haurangi and Oaks huts are available for booking. The huts have mattresses, cooking facilities, plates, cups and utensils and cost between $40 and $100 per night, depending on bunk capacity.
Alternative route Fit, experienced walkers could chose to return to the carpark using either the McKerrow or Cattle Ridge tracks. Used in conjunction with the Orongorongo Track, either of these tracks will take 5–6 hours return (both tracks are medium grade). Alternatively, a shorter walk is the Catchpool Loop Track, which follows the Orongorongo Track for 15 minutes before looping back on the opposite side of the Catchpool Valley (allow 45 minutes return).
Information DOC Wellington Visitor Centre Tel: 04-384-7770, Email: wellingtonvc@doc.govt.nz

Above and opposite *Forest on the Orongorongo Track, Rimutaka Forest Park*

TARARUA FOREST PARK, WAIRARAPA
SMITH CREEK & TAWHARENIKAU RIVER

Smith Creek is an attractive tributary of the Tawharenikau River in the southern part of Tararua Forest Park. While a very pleasant return amble into the Tawhareninkau Valley using the Smith Creek Track is the least strenuous option (and the one most suitable for families and walkers with modest ambitions), two alternatives routes are also described here. The first is a round trip called the Dobson Loop Track that will suit energetic walkers. The second is a through trip following the Tawharenikau River down a long gorge that suits experienced trampers who enjoy a good soaking. Note that on modern maps the river appears spelt incorrectly as 'Tauherenikau'.

Kaitoke to Smith Creek Shelter via old Dobson Hut site 2.5–3 hours

From the Kaitoke carpark the Puffer Track climbs through regenerating bush, with native plants slowly replacing spiky gorse. Well-benched and gravelled, the track wends its way upwards for 20–30 minutes before reaching a signposted junction. Take the left fork indicating the way to Marchant Ridge and Alpha Hut. Now on the ridge crest, the track ascends slowly but surely until reaching another track junction at the site of the old Dobson Hut, the sole remains of which is an old concrete chimney.

Take the track leading downhill past the site towards the Tawharenikau Valley, following a steepish spur between Fell and Canyon Creeks. The gradient doesn't ease until the flats of the valley floor beside Smith Creek. Head downvalley at a track junction and cross Canyon Creek to reach Smith Creek Shelter. This is a larger affair than the term 'shelter' suggests: it was once a well-used hut built by the Wellington Tramping & Mountaineering Club, but during the 1980s it suffered constant vandalism. Consequently, the windows and doors were removed, converting it into a partially open shelter. Nearby tracks lead into the open riverbed of the Tawharenikau, a pleasant place for skipping stones or having lunch.

Tawharenikau River gorge, Tararua Forest Park

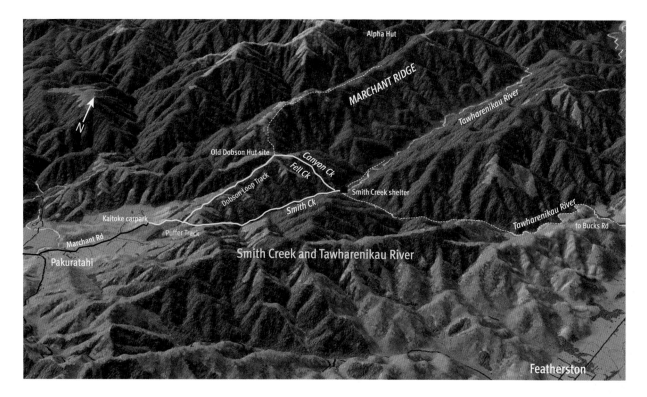

Smith Creek and Tawharenikau River

Smith Creek to Kaitoke carpark 1.5–2 hours

From the shelter, head back up the Smith Creek Track. This well-benched and gently climbing track is a delight, passing under innumerable tree ferns that hang overhead like a tunnel in places. The nice gradient is rudely interrupted by one detour around a slip, but otherwise remains pleasant ambling until a major fork in the Smith Creek headwaters. Here the track ascends sharply up a staircase of roots, cresting the ridge at Puffer Saddle. An easy downhill walk leads back to the carpark.

Kaitoke to Tawharenikau Gorge via Smith Creek Track 6–8 hours

Although requiring some transport juggling, a scramble down the Tawharenikau is the perfect introduction to Tararua gorges. Low river levels and a good forecast are essential, and wetsuits come highly recommended even during summer.

From Kaitoke take the Smith Creek Track to Smith Creek Shelter (described in reverse direction above). Find one of several tracks leading to the open rocky bed of the Tawharenikau

River, and follow it downstream. The gorge begins where the river swings hard eastwards. Travel involves hopping down the boulder-strewn gorge, crossing the river , and scrambling around deep pools. No compulsory swims occur until about two-thirds of the way through (although floods can alter the nature of the gorge). Where the river opens out and some pine trees and power lines come into view, watch for a unmarked track that exits on the true right, ending at Bucks Road, some 6 kilometres from Featherston.

Grade Easy (Smith Creek return), Medium (Dobson Loop Track), Hard (Tawharenikau Gorge)

Maps S26 Carterton, Tararua Recreation map ·

Total Walking Time Smith Creek Return, 3–4 hours; Dobson Loop Track, 4–6 hours; Tawharenikau Gorge, 6–8 hours.

Access Access is from Marchant Road, 14 km north of Upper Hutt on SH 2.

Information DOC Wellington Visitor Centre Tel: 04-384-7770, Email: wellingtonvc@doc.govt.nz

WELLINGTON
KAPITI ISLAND NATURE RESERVE

Kaka, Kapiti Island

The largest island (1965 hectares) in the Wellington area, Kapiti Island rises out of the sea like a misshapen loaf of bread; a forest fortress home to some of the country's most endangered birds including takahe, tieke (saddleback), hihi (stitchbird), kaka, and kokako. More common birds including tui, bellbirds, robins, kereru and pukeko also abound on the island.

At various times it has been the stronghold of feared Maori warrior Te Rauparaha, a base for whalers plying Cook Strait, a failed farming venture, and one of the country's first nature reserves (established in 1897): the island's fascinating history has been well documented in Chris Maclean's superb book, Kapiti. Visitors to the island will enjoy reading about the truly heroic efforts made by a long succession of people to convert the island from a pest-infested place of denuded forests to the thriving bird sanctuary it is today.

Five kilometres west of Paraparaumu, the island is just 20 minutes by launch from the mainland, making it the country's most accessible nature reserve. Visitors to the island require a permit, easily obtained from DOC.

Rangatira Point to Tuteremoana Trig via Trig and Wilkinson Tracks 3–4 hours return

After disembarking at the stony beach of Rangatira Point and assembling at the shelter, a guide will provide a brief introduction to the island – including current track conditions – before you can explore by yourself. Two tracks, the Wilkinson and Trig Tracks, both start from Rangatira Point near the site of the historic whare, and climb through mature forest on the eastern slopes of the island. About three-quarters of the way up, the two tracks meet to form a single track that leads to the top of the island, a point called Tuteremoana (521 m). A viewing tower here offers great views down sheer cliffs on the island's western side and over to the Kapiti coast. On clear days Mt Taranaki and the South Island are visible too.

Descend back to the junction and take the alternative track to the one you ascended to make a partial round trip. The Wilkinson Track's more gradual gradient is kinder on the knees for a descent.

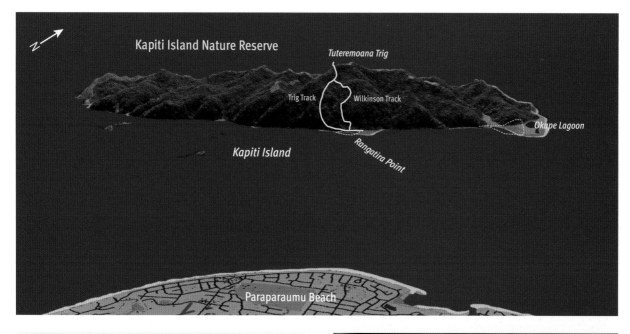

Kapiti Island Nature Reserve

Tuteremoana Trig

Trig Track   Wilkinson Track

Kapiti Island

Rangatira Point

Okupe Lagoon

Paraparaumu Beach

Grade Easy–Medium

Map R26 Paraparaumu

Total Walking Time 3–4 hours return

Access Kapiti Island is accessible from Paraparaumu Beach, off SH 1 north of Wellington. To visit the island you must obtain a permit from DOC in Wellington ($9 for adults, $4.50 for children). During summer months and weekends there is heavy demand for the limited number of permits, so apply in advance. DOC can also provide information on the operators who are licensed to run boat trips out to the island; these must also be booked in advance, after you have received your permit. Most trips to Kapiti last from 9 am to 3 pm.

Alternative route Walkers wanting an undemanding stroll with plenty of time to observe birds will enjoy the flat tracks that encircle Rangatira Flat (30 minutes round trip). At the north end of Kapiti Island, two loop walks exist around Okupe Lagoon. These walks are only available to those who choose to be dropped off by the launch at the North End, rather than Rangatira Point.

Information DOC Wellington Visitor Centre Tel: 04-384-7770, Email: wellingtonvc@doc.govt.nz

Weka, Kapiti Island

PORIRUA, WELLINGTON
COLONIAL KNOB WALKWAY

Wellington's location at the junction of several major faultlines ensures a hilly nature ideally suited to walkers who like good viewpoints. Mt Kaukau, Mt Victoria, Makara Peak and Belmont Trig all compete with Colonial Knob as arguably the best viewpoint in the city environs. At 458 metres Colonial Knob is the highest point in the hills of western Wellington, and the views certainly prove panoramic.

Timing a walk to arrive on top during evening can be particularly rewarding: the sun sinks over the Marlborough Sounds, alpenglow creeps over the bulky pyramid of Mt Tapuae-o-Uenuku and on exceptionally clear days the graceful cone of Mt Taranaki rises to the northwest. Dusky light glints off Porirua Harbour to the north, and the entrance of Wellington Harbour appears to the south. The Tararua and Rimutaka ranges span the eastern horizon, while the northern suburbs of Wellington sprawl in the foreground. Closer are the kneaded hills above Mill Creek, looking like plaited bread.

While the 370 metre ascent will deter some walkers, the Colonial Knob Walkway will suit those of modest fitness who don't mind hills. It climbs through mature kohekohe–tawa forest to emerge onto open farmland and finally the summit itself. While completing a loop back to Broken Hill Road is possible using part of a vehicle track over farmland, the recently graded road proves ugly and unrewarding. Unless you have a strong aversion to retracing your footsteps, it is better to return back over the main track.*

Broken Hill Road to Colonial Knob 1.5–2 hours

The carpark for the Colonial Knob Walkway begins off Broken Hill Road, near a refuse tip right in the centre of industrial Porirua. While not a promising start, the walk soon proves well worthwhile. Cross a footbridge over Mitchell Stream to a DOC information panel. It's worth studying the map here, as there are a potentially confusing number of tracks in the lower area, which passes through the Spicer Botanical Park. Follow the Australis Walk, past a grassy picnic area, through an avenue of eucalypt and acacia trees and across the Mitchell Stream on a second footbridge. Here, follow

Evening over Kapiti Island and the western Wellington hills from Colonial Knob

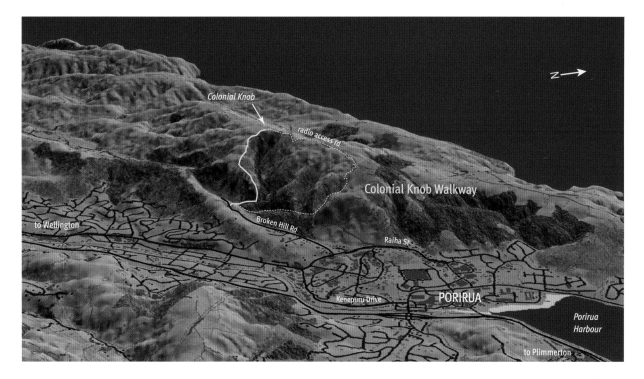

the poles with the orange walkway symbol across a third bridge over the stream where a sign marks the beginning of the Colonial Knob Scenic Reserve (still just 5 minutes from the carpark).

The track enters dense forest soon afterward, to reach an un-signposted track junction after 1 minute. Head left, over a bridge spanning a tributary of Mitchell Stream. The track sidles upvalley, curls around past an old disused water reservoir (built to service Porirua Hospital in the 19th century), and begins a gentle ascent to reach a signposted track junction. Head left, to where the real climbing begins.

The track, recently re-benched and gravelled, with drainage ditches and sections of wooden stairs, looks a bit raw but give it a few years and the ferns and moss will reclaim the banks to leave a beautifully graded path. It zigzags uphill through some lush, shady native forest. Finally, past some large macrocarpa trees, the track emerges out of the forest to cross a stile onto private farmland. Wooden marker poles lead up over grassy slopes, wend over hillsides and

finally climb along the farm ridge with increasingly good views over Porirua and the Belmont hills.

After crossing a second stile, the last section winds upward on a freshly-gravelled track to a short steep pinch to the trig station which surmounts Colonial Knob. A radio mast dominates the next knoll north.

Grade Easy–Medium
Maps R27, R28 Wellington
Total Walking Time 3–4 hours return
Access The Colonial Knob Walkway lies in the Wellington suburb of Porirua. Exit SH 1 to Porirua City (20 km north of Wellington city). At the first major roundabout in Porirua city, turn left onto Kenepuru Drive. After 2 km turn right onto Raiha Street, and left onto Broken Hill Road after a further 500 metres. The carpark is well signposted, about 1.2 km up the road.
Information DOC Wellington Visitor Centre Tel: 04-384-7770, Email: wellingtonvc@doc.govt.nz

WELLINGTON
MAKARA WALKWAY

Makara Beach lies west of Wellington, a stony curve of beach set between imposing headlands that has long been a favourite weekend retreat for city dwellers. The Makara Walkway climbs from the west end of Makara Beach over one of these headlands, up to the site of some World War II gun emplacements, set with a commanding view over Cook Strait. Northwards lies the tabletop of Mana Island, obscuring all but the lumpy backbone of Kapiti Island, while westwards the Marlborough Sounds rise over the other side of the strait, barely 30 kilometres away. After descending to Opau Bay (a place for picnics and swimming) a route loops back to Makara Beach following the coastline. Crossing a mixture of farmland and coastal environments, the walkway will suit families with school-age children and walkers of moderate fitness.

Makara Beach to Opau Bay via Gun Emplacement
1.5–2 hours

A well-defined gravel path leads along the coast, popular with fishers, picnickers, and divers, before rounding one small headland to Wharehou Bay. From the western end of Wharehou Bay a junction marks the start of the track to the gun emplacements (note that this section is closed from 1 August to 31 October for lambing). The track climbs grassy slopes up to the ridge above a headland, once occupied by a Maori pa. From here the walkway follows the narrow ridgeline, largely following a fence, with the views expanding as height is gained. This part of the track is largely un-formed and footing can be uneven in places, and parents will need to watch children near the steep slopes above the sea.

At the crest of the ridge, now 201 metres above sea level, the track crosses a stile and sidles to the remains of the gun emplacements. Fort Opau, manned by 100 sol-diers between 1941 and 1943, had two guns with a range halfway across Cook Strait. The expected Japanese invasion never came, and the guns were removed in 1944. The two main concrete bunkers are fenced (and off limits due to their instability) but a bench seat is conveniently placed for admiring views. From the bunkers, a broad grassy track leads over a lip, and passes the concrete foundations of

Driftwood teepee, Opau Bay, Makara Walkway

Terawhiti Hill

KARORI

Opau Strm

Ohau Point

Makara Rd

gun emplacements

Opau Bay

Makara Walkway

Makara Beach

Wharehou Bay

N

what were soldiers' barracks. Shortly beyond, branch right at a signposted junction onto an old sealed road, its surface largely claimed by potholes and lichens. After a 25–30 minute walk the road ends at the muddy trickle of Opau Stream. Follow the true left bank for 200–300 metres, and through a barricade of driftwood to reach stony Opau Bay.

Opau Bay to Makara Beach via coastline
1.5–2 hours

From Opau Bay the route simply follows the coastline, with pebbly stones underfoot and rocky reefs offshore. Here, the sifting action of the sea, aided by the relentless northerlies, has sorted rocks according to size, and they roll in an ankle-wrenching fashion in places. Native plants – prostrate shrubs cuffed by the sea – intermingle with prickly exotics, and the place has a rough, wild charm. Look for pied shags, variable oystercatchers, terns and white-faced herons en route. A formed route begins again on the far side of the headland at Wharehou Bay, and soon joins the main trail back to Makara.

Grade Easy–Medium
Maps R27, R28 Wellington
Total Walking Time 3–4 hours round trip
Access Roads lead through the Wellington suburb of Karori, where the Makara Road branches off. While sealed, the 16 km Makara Road is narrow and requires care; allow about a 30 minute drive from Wellington. There are toilets at the carpark.
Information DOC Wellington Visitor Centre Tel: 04-384-7770, Email: wellingtonvc@doc.govt.nz

PUPONGA FARM PARK, GOLDEN BAY
WHARARIKI BEACH

Wharariki Beach offers walkers one of the most dramatic and wild coasts in Golden Bay; an area which abounds in attractive and often undeveloped coastlines. While in recent years the once obscure walk has become very popular, the beach is large enough to find solitude, and is certainly worthy of a few hours exploration. Wharariki includes large sand dunes, fur seals, and narrow caves in the headland, but its most impressive feature is the aptly-named Archway Islands, lying just offshore.

Carpark to Wharariki Beach 20–30 minutes
From the carpark, cross a stile over the fence and follow poles leading over hilly farmland. Once over a grassy rise the track descends through a small patch of coastal forest to emerge onto sand dunes dominated by marram grass. Through the dunes, footprints lead to the beach, with the mound-shaped headland prominent ahead. At low tide walkers can enter some narrow fissures in the headland, or

Dawn over the Archway Islands, Wharariki Beach

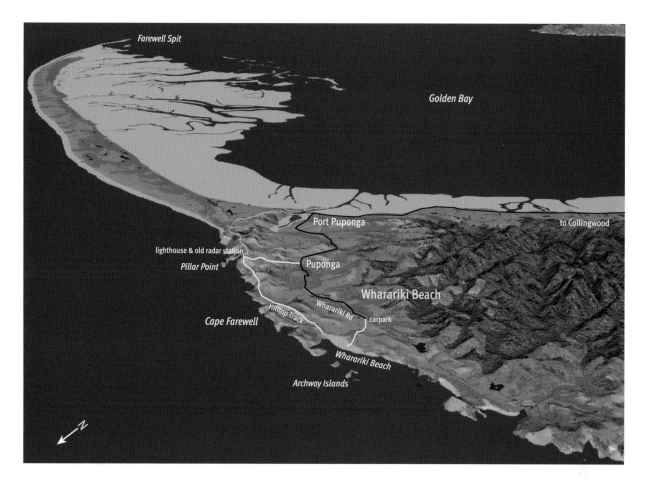

Farewell Spit

Golden Bay

Port Puponga

to Collingwood

lighthouse & old radar station

Pillar Point

Puponga

Wharariki Beach

Cape Farewell

Hilltop Track

Wharariki Rd

carpark

Wharariki Beach

Archway Islands

watch fur seals in the sheltered pools nearby. The arches of the Archway Islands are not at first obvious, but open out dramatically on the walk west along the beach.

Wharariki Beach to Pillar Point and Wharariki Road 2.5 hours

At mid-tide or lower, walkers can reach the Hilltop Track from the eastern end of Wharariki Beach. This winds up over farmland and scrub, past spectacular views over the cliffs of Cape Farewell, and beyond to a lighthouse at Pillar Point. Ruins of a World War II radar station lie nearby. From Pillar Point a vehicle track leads back to a carpark on Wharariki Road. A 2 kilometre walk along the road leads back to your vehicle.

Grade Easy–Medium
Maps M24 Farewell, Kahurangi Parkmap
Total Walking Time 3.5–4 hours
Access From Takaka follow SH 60 to Port Puponga, near the base of Farewell Spit. Head left along Wharariki Road for 4 km to the carpark.
Alternative route From Pillar Point, more energetic walkers can follow the Hilltop Walk along the Old Man Range to Port Puponga, which is some 4 km from the Wharariki Road carpark.
Information DOC Takaka Tel: 03-525-8444

ABEL TASMAN NATIONAL PARK
TOTARANUI TO SEPARATION POINT • TAUPO POINT

TOTARANUI TO SEPARATION POINT

The Abel Tasman Coast Track, one of DOC's Great Walks, is a 4–5 day tramp connecting Wainui Inlet with Marahau. Walkers can take advantage of the many road and water taxi access points to enjoy shorter sections of the track.

Totaranui has long been a favourite camping spot for holidaymakers over the summer, and is an excellent place from which to enjoy several good day walks. Perhaps the best of these is the walk to Separation Point, famous as the headland which separates Golden and Tasman bays. Fine coastal forest

and exquisite beaches make this a superb walk, and in autumn or winter walkers can enjoy watching fur seals at Separation Point. Both Anapai Bay and Mutton Cove have campsites.

Totaranui to Anapai Bay 1 hour

From Totaranui the main Abel Tasman Coast Track skirts the estuary on the northern side of Totaranui Beach. On the far side of the estuary, the track climbs over a low saddle and down through some of the most verdant forest in Abel Tasman National Park to Anapai Bay. With its statuesque

Abel Tasman's famous golden sand, Totaranui. Photo: Darryn Pegram/Black Robin Photography

Totaranui to Separation Point

granite pillars, golden sands and intimate shape, Anapai Bay is arguably the finest of all those on the Coast Track.

Anapai Bay to Separation Point 1.5 hours

After departing Anapai Bay, the track skirts more beaches and rocky headlands to reach Mutton Cove in 30 minutes. From Mutton Cove the main Abel Tasman Coast Track heads inland, over to Whariwharangi Bay. Ignore this, and instead head north along the track to Separation Point, which requires some scrambling at the end. A lighthouse, granite cliffs and savage tides characterise the point, as does the presence of New Zealand fur seals. The seals, mainly adult males or juveniles, migrate here from other breeding colonies to winter over. A few stragglers sometimes remain over summer. Avoid approaching fur seals too closely.

Grade Medium

Map Abel Tasman Parkmap

Total Walking Time 5–6 hours return

Access From Marahau catch a water taxi to Totaranui. From Takaka drive over the Abel Tasman Drive to Wainui Inlet, then take Totaranui Road to Totaranui, where there is a large camping area, toilets, and an information shelter.

Alternative route From Separation Point energetic walkers could return to Totaranui via Whariwharangi Bay and Gibbs Hill. This takes a full day of some 7–8 hours, and walkers will need to carry water over the Gibbs Hill section.

Information DOC Takaka Tel: 03-525-8444

Above *Taupo Point. Photo: Darryn Pegram/Black Robin Photography* **Opposite** *Low tide at Wainui Inlet, Golden Bay.*

TAUPO POINT

Whether it is geology or history or simply fine coastal scenery that attracts you, the unusual headland of Taupo Point is a spot worth visiting. Granite dominates almost the entire coastline of Abel Tasman National Park, except at Taupo Point, which comprises limestone, a rock type better known in Canaan in the interior of the park.

Taupo Point also has a rich Maori history. Nearby Whariwharangi Bay is thought to be the place where Dutch seafarer Abel Tasman had a bloody encounter with Maori in 1642, and it may be that the waka which paddled out to his ships originated from Taupo Point. Certainly, a Maori pa once dominated the point, which made a superb, easily-defended vantage point.

Takapou Bay Carpark to Taupo Point 1 hour

Take the main Abel Tasman Coast Track for 5 minutes, until the signposted side track to Taupo Point branches off. The track follows the rocky coast northwards, climbing around Uarau Point, then descending to the coastline on the far side. Easy travel leads along beaches, and past a rocky reef to Taupo Point. There is a camping and picnic area on the sandy isthmus which connects the point to the mainland. Here, a small Maori village, or kainga, once existed. A track lead to the Point's summit, which offers broad views across Golden Bay as far as Farewell Spit.

Grade Easy
Map Abel Tasman Parkmap
Total Walking Time 2–2.5 hours return
Access From Takaka, take Abel Tasman Drive to Wainui Bay as far as Anatimo, then turn off onto McShane Road. At Takapou Bay there is a carpark, information shelter and toilets, marking the start of the Abel Tasman Coast Track.
Alternative route Energetic and experienced walkers can traverse the untracked coastline north of Taupo Point as far as Whariwharangi Hut, and return to the carpark on the Abel Tasman Coast Track. This would take a very full day, and must be planned around low tide. Rock scrambling is necessary in places.
Information DOC Takaka Tel: 03-525-8444

ABEL TASMAN NATIONAL PARK
TE PUKATEA BAY & PITT HEAD

One of the most scenic locations in the southern half of Abel Tasman National Park is that around Anchorage. Anchorage is a meeting place for all those who enjoy the park: trampers, walkers, sea kayakers, yachties and boaties. From Anchorage, an excellent track leads over to the picturesque Te Pukatea Bay, and then north around Pitt Head to loop back to the start.

Anchorage to Te Pukatea Bay 30 minutes

Set back from Anchorage beach is a large DOC hut used by walkers on the Abel Tasman Coast Track. From the nearby campsite, a track leads over a bridge then up a low, forested saddle to Te Puketea Bay. A perfect golden-sand crescent, the bay makes a fine place to picnic or swim, and there is also a campsite. Head northwards along the beach to pick up the track to Pitt Head.

Te Pukatea Bay to Anchorage via Pitt Head 1 hour

A well-benched track wends its way through regenerating forest, chiefly kanuka, up to a lookout at Pitt Head. The headland's steep sides and narrow approach made it a natural vantage point for Maori, who built a fortified pa here. From the lookout point, the track curls around the northern part of the headland through forest back to Anchorage.

Grade Easy
Map Abel Tasman Parkmap
Total Walking Time 1.5 hours return
Access Catch a water taxi from Marahau to Anchorage.
Alternative route From Anchorage, the walk to Watering Cove makes another enjoyable option (1.5 hours return). Instead of returning by water taxi, walkers can follow the Abel Tasman Coast Track from Anchorage to Marahau. This would add a further 4–5 hours.
Information DOC Motueka Tel: 03-528-1810

Walkers, Te Pukatea Bay

Marahau

Abel Tasman Coast Track

Apple Tree Bay

Te Pukatea Bay and Pitt Head

water taxi

Adele Island

Anchorage Hut

The Anchorage

Torrent Bay

Falls River

Te Pukatea Bay

Pitt Head

Torrent Bay

Bark Bay

Dawn, Te Pukatea Bay

KAHURANGI NATIONAL PARK
LAKE SYLVESTER & THE LOCKETT RANGE • ASBESTOS COTTAGE • MT ARTHUR & THE TABLELAND • LODESTONE

LAKE SYLVESTER AND THE LOCKETT RANGE

Separating the Cobb Valley from the Waingaro River, the Lockett Range is quintessential Kahurangi tops: rolling tussock grasslands, lakes and tarns galore, and interesting – but not daunting – mountains. Lake Sylvester is one of the larger lakes on the range, nestled in a hollow on the tops above Sylvester Hut.

Although involving a solid 500 metre ascent, which is steep in places, the track to Sylvester Hut follows an old disused vehicle track and so offers respite on a number of zigzags and flatter sections. It makes an easy overnight destination, or a more challenging day walk.

Cobb Reservoir Road to Sylvester Hut (12 bunks, wood stove, $10/night) 2–2.5 hours

From the penstocks, a track leads through forest on the true left side of the Cobb Reservoir. After 40 minutes or so, the track turns northward, climbing onto a spur south of Galena Creek. It zigzags up a steeper section until gaining more moderate slopes above. Higher up, subalpine shrubs replace forest, and the angle eases again for the final stretch to Sylvester Hut. This is one of the newer DOC huts, replacing the older Bushline Hut built in 1953. It offers grand views over the Cobb Valley and across to the neighbouring Peel Range.

Sylvester Hut to Lake Sylvester 30 minutes return

Lake Sylvester is a simple stroll up a broad tussock basin. In summer walkers can enjoy swimming in its cool waters. During the 1950s the lake level was artificially raised to supplement water levels for the main Cobb power scheme.

Those who still have energy might like to walk around the lake's southern shores and beyond to Iron Lake, or even as far as Iron Hill (about 3 hours return from Sylvester Hut).

> **Grade** Medium
> **Maps** M26 Cobb, Kahurangi Parkmap
> **Total Walking Time** 4–6 hours return
> **Access** From Upper Takaka take the Cobb Dam Road. Where the road reaches the reservoir, head right along to the penstocks and beyond to a carpark.
> **Information** DOC Takaka Tel: 03-525-8444

ASBESTOS COTTAGE

Some tracks prove satisfying not only for their scenery, but because they have a compelling human story behind them. Asbestos Cottage lies in the bush-clad hills of the upper Takaka Valley, and is reached on an undemanding track from the road into the Cobb Valley. The historic hut, probably built sometime between 1890 and 1900, was for nearly 40 years the home of Annie and Henry Chaffey.

Both came to live in the mountains in 1913 as a means of escaping previous lives: Annie from an unhappy marriage, and Henry from a divorce and the demons of life in town. The couple first occupied another nearby hut, but moved to Asbestos Cottage in 1915. From there Henry prospected the surrounding mountains, developed an asbestos mine, and lugged supplies in from Takaka or Mouteka. Annie made jam, kept house, entertained guests (which included the occasional tramper) and stayed put. She left the cottage only twice: once (temporarily) after an illness, and finally after Henry died of a heart attack in 1951. Annie adapted poorly to life in town and took her own life two years later.

Compulsory reading for anyone who enjoys this walk is Jim Henderson's excellent 1981 book about their lives, The Exiles of Asbestos Cottage: *'Surely New Zealand's history knows no stranger love affair than this, the true story of rock-like resolution and sorrow of the Exiles of Asbestos Cottage.'*

Iron Hill (1695m)

LOCKETT RANGE

Iron Lake

Lake Sylvester

Sylvester Hut

Lake Sylvester Track

Galena Ck

penstocks

Cobb River

Cobb Reservoir

Cobb Dam Road

hydro station

Takaka River

Asbestos Cottage Track

Gabbro Ck

Asbestos Ck

Asbestos Cottage

asbestos mine

Camp Ck

TABLELAND

Takaka River

Flora Strm

Lodestone (1462m)

Gordons Pyramid

Quartz Ck

Lodestone Track

Flora Hut

Flora Saddle

Mt Arthur Hut

Mt Arthur (1795m)

Flora carpark

Mt Arthur Track

Graham Valley Road

N

Carpark to Asbestos Mine 1 hour

The walk in to Asbestos Cottage follows an old road pushed in to develop Chaffey's asbestos mine in the late 1940s. It meanders amongst lush podocarp–beech forest for 35 minutes before diverting onto a narrower track around a slip that has taken out a section of the old road. A couple of streams offer drinking water en route.

Another 30 minutes walking leads to a ford of Gabbro Creek, and the mine site just beyond. An old oven, abandoned boots, glass bottles, and bits of mining machinery litter the site, and nearby the track opens out into what was the main area for extracting ore. This is a surreal gash of greenish substrate in the earth, fringed by regenerating manuka.

Mine to Asbestos Cottage (4 bunks, open fire, $5/night) 30 minutes

From the mine, red marker poles lead through manuka into more substantial forest and up a steeper, rocky path. Once across Asbestos Creek on a footbridge, the track sidles along slopes to reach Camp Creek and Asbestos Cottage, set in a bracken-filled clearing. Information panels inside the hut detail its history and that of the Chaffeys.

Thanks to the efforts of the former NZ Forest Service and DOC, Asbestos Cottage remains in good condition. Jack McBurney of the NZFS replaced the rotting malthoid roof with corrugated iron in the 1960s, and made other repairs. Then in 1997 ex-NZFS ranger Max Polglaze undertook more extensive restoration with carpenter Gregor Koolen.

Grade Easy
Maps M26 Cobb, M27 Mount Arthur, Kahurangi Parkmap
Total Walking Time 3 hours return
Access From Upper Takaka, take the winding Cobb Dam Road for some 20 km. The signposted start of the Asbestos Cottage track is about 3km past the Hydro Station.
Alternative route From Asbestos Cottage it is possible to walk through to Flora Carpark via the Upper Takaka Valley and Flora Track. This takes about 4 hours.
Information DOC Takaka Tel: 03-525-8444

MT ARTHUR AND THE TABLELAND

Mt Arthur (1795 m) forms a distinctive domed summit on Nelson's western skyline. A mountain composed entirely of marble (a particular form of limestone), it is part of a sequence beginning around the Takaka Hill and stretching as far south as Mt Owen (the park's highest peak). Like the latter peak, Mt Arthur offers walkers a rare glimpse of marble patterned and striated by past glaciation. Both peaks are also honeycombed with sinkholes and caves, some of the most extensive in the Southern Hemisphere. During summer Mt Arthur abounds with alpine plants.

Despite its geological interest, most walkers enjoy Mt Arthur simply because it is one of Kahurangi's most accessible summits, and offers outstanding views. The walk starts at the Flora carpark, which due to its lofty 940 metre altitude ensures the mountain is more than half-climbed before you begin.

Whilst in benign weather the tramp to the summit of Mt Arthur is a relatively simple excursion, be aware that the summit is exposed, and winter ascents usually require ice axes and crampons.

Flora Carpark to Mt Arthur Hut (8 bunks, gas heater, $10/night) 1–1.5 hours

At the Flora carpark, a shelter facing Mt Arthur provides information on the area's natural and human history. The wide track (once a vehicle track) climbs gently to a signposted junction at Flora Saddle. At the saddle take the signposted track heading left towards Mt Arthur Hut. More gentle climbing through beech forest leads into a section of *Dracophyllum* and beyond to the hut, nestled near the edge of the bush.

Mt Arthur Hut to Mt Arthur Summit 3–4 hours return

Behind Mt Arthur the track soon passes the last of the forest and emerges onto the tops. From here a poled route leads through subalpine plants and across bands of interesting marble. Beware that under winter snow, sinkholes can be obscured.

A signpost indicates the turnoff to Gordons Pyramid. The main route to Mt Arthur continues gently upwards for a while until the ridge steepens. Poles then lead through marble faces on the mountain's northern slopes, until finally gaining the broad, rounded summit of Mt Arthur. From the tops, much of Kahurangi National Park lies before you, with the Tableland prominent in the foreground. Eastwards lie the Waimea Basin and Tasman Bay.

Grade Medium
Maps M27 Mt Arthur, Kahurangi Parkmap
Total Walking Time 5–7 hours
Access From Ngatimoti, on the highway connecting Motueka and Tapawera, turn onto the Motueka River West Bank Road. The Graham Valley Road branches off a few kilometres south of here. Flora carpark is reached after a steep and winding drive.
Alternative route From Mt Arthur Hut walkers can take the track to Flora Hut, which provides an alternative route back to the Flora Carpark. Add an extra 30 minutes for this route.
Information DOC Motueka Tel: 03-528-9117

LODESTONE

Lodestone, a tiny island of subalpine tops amongst a sea of almost uniform beech forest, is one of several small peaks at the northern end of the Arthur Range. The peak provides an alternative, shorter day walk to Mt Arthur, beginning also from the Flora Carpark. Although the scenery does not match the diversity of that of Mt Arthur, Lodestone's summit (1462 m) also offers excellent views.

Flora Carpark to Lodestone 2 hours
The signposted track to Lodestone begins immediately from the Flora carpark, climbing stiffly through beech trees onto a small, forested knoll. After a brief flat section, more climbing leads onto a narrow, undulating ridge which steepens again just before the bushline. As well as magnificent views of Mt Arthur and Gordons Pyramid, the summit offers a broad panorama of Tasman Bay and the Waimea basin.

Lodestone to Flora Carpark via Flora Hut (12 bunks, open fire, $5/night) 1.5–2 hours
Poles lead over the summit to the bushline on Lodestone's southwestern corner, where a track leads down a forested ridge. The ridge ends at the confluence of Quartz Creek and Flora Stream. Ford the stream to reach Flora Hut, where picnic tables provide convenient places for a rest and snack. From the hut a further 30 minute walk leads back to the carpark.

Grade Medium
Maps M27 Mount Arthur, Kahurangi Parkmap
Total Walking Time 3.5–4 hours
Access From Ngatimoti, on the highway connecting Motueka and Tapawera, turn onto the Motueka River West Bank Road. The Graham Valley Road branches off a few kilometres south of here. Flora carpark is reached after a steep and winding drive.
Information DOC Motueka Tel: 03-528-9117

Sunrise over Gordon's Pyramid from near Mt Arthur Hut

NELSON LAKES NATIONAL PARK
BUSHLINE HUT & MT ROBERT • LAKE ROTOITI

BUSHLINE HUT AND MT ROBERT

The rounded knoll of Mt Robert (1421 m) dominates Lake Rotoiti when viewed from Kerr Bay. Named by geologist and explorer Julius von Haast, the mountain was scorched of its original vegetation by an accidental fire in 1887, and was later kept clear for grazing by deliberate fires. Grazing eventually proved uneconomic and vegetation is very slowly reclothing the mountain.

A very agreeable round trip climbs the northern faces of the mountain to the superbly located Bushline Hut, and beyond to the summit of Mt Robert itself. Excellent views and a variety of bush and tops scenery add to its appeal. Whilst in benign weather the section between Bushline Hut and Mt Robert proves straightforward, it is very exposed to bad weather, and winter ascents may require an ice axe and crampons.

Mt Robert Road to Bushline Hut (14 bunks, wood burner, $10/night) 2–2.5 hours

From the carpark, the trail to Bushline Hut – known as Paddys Track – is clearly signposted, and skirts above the artificially low bushline of Mt Robert, crossing in and out of numerous guts, where shrubby native plants are making a comeback amongst the grasses. The track enters forest again for a short stretch. Shortly after crossing Robert Stream the track begins to climb in a series of zigzags, rounds the broad shoulder of Pt 1098 m, then begins the last ascent to Bushline Hut. At an altitude of 1300 metres, the hut has fine views over St Arnaud and Lake Rotoiti, and as far as the mountains of the Richmond Range and Kahurangi National Park.

Bushline Hut to Mt Robert and Carpark via Pinchgut Track 2–2.5 hours

From Bushline Hut the well-graded Paddys Track leads up a broad, rounded spur, soon passing a couple of private ski huts. Be sure to carry plenty of water as there is none available along the route. Paddys Track joins the main Robert Ridge route at Relax Shelter, just a few hundred metres south of Mt Robert itself. After enjoying the views from Mt Robert, drop down to Bushedge Shelter. This offers some respite from the elements during inclement weather or a shady spot for lunch.

From the shelter the track begins a steep, zigzagging descent, initially through stunted beech forest, then out onto more exposed slopes, before returning to the forest and ending abruptly at the carpark.

Grade Medium–Hard
Maps N29 St Arnaud, Nelson Lakes Parkmap
Total Walking Time 4–5 hours
Access The alpine township of St Arnaud lies on SH 63. The turnoff to the Mt Robert Road is 2 km west of the township. The carpark is a further 5 km. During the peak summer season shuttles service the area.
Alternative route The trip can easily be done in reverse, which involves a steeper ascent and gentler descent.
Information DOC St Arnaud Tel: 03-521-1806

LAKE ROTOITI

Rotoiti is the more accessible of the two lakes from which Nelson Lakes National Park takes its name. Carved by glaciation during the last ice age, it is a deep lake, fed by the Travers River which drains the mountains at the lakehead.

Since 1997 the eastern shores of the lake have been the site of DOC's ambitious and successful Rotoiti Nature Recovery Project. Originally just 825 hectares, the project has been extended to cover around 5000 hectares. Intensive pest control (mainly of wasps, rats, stoats and possums) is ensuring not only good survival for the area's existing native animals, but also the exciting possibility of introducing lost species. Great spotted kiwi were reintroduced in 2004, and there are hopes of adding saddleback (tieke) and yellowhead (mohua) in the future.

Keen walkers can use tracks that almost circumnavigate the lake, beginning from Kerr Bay. Although reasonably flat and straightforward, the entire walk will occupy a full day. For those wanting a shorter, half-day walk, a water taxi pick-up can be arranged for either the Lake Head or Coldwater jetties.

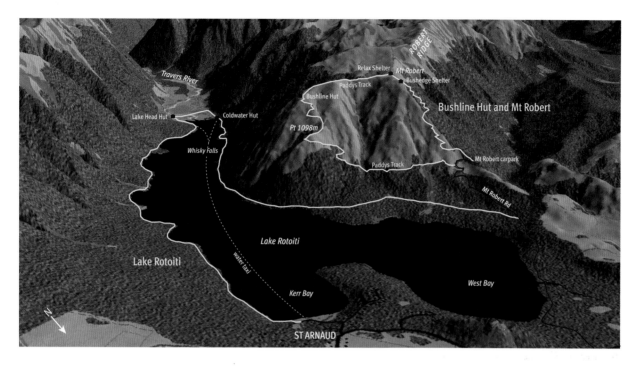

Kerr Bay to Lake Head Hut (30 bunks, wood stove, $10/night) 3 hours

From Kerr Bay the flat, easy Lake Head Track follows the eastern shores of Lake Rotoiti, passing through beech forests of often vibrant birdlife, thanks to DOC's efforts. Look out for honeydew on the trunks of beech trees, a waste product of the scale insect favoured by bellbirds and tui.

Although the track stays mainly in the forest, there are frequent opportunities for lakeside viewpoints. During summer, sandflies can be annoying. The lake narrows near its head, and about 20 minutes after passing the Lake Head jetty the trail reaches Lake Head Hut.

Lake Head Hut to Coldwater Hut (6 bunks, open fire, $5/night) 30–40 minutes

From the hut, a poled route leads across the grassy river flats of the lower valley to the Travers River. Continuing the tramp around to the western shores of Lake Rotoiti is dependent on crossing the unbridged Travers River, which is impossible after significant rainfall, but easy enough in normal conditions. Once across on the true left bank, pick up a track which meanders through beech forest to Coldwater Hut.

Coldwater Hut to Mt Robert Road 3–4 hours

From Coldwater Hut the track skirts the slopes on the western side of Lake Rotoiti, providing pleasant undulating tramping. Whisky Falls offers a diversion after about 90 minutes. Where the lake begins to broaden, the track departs the shore and heads through flattish, forested terrain to finally end at the Mt Robert Road, a 20 minute walk from the carpark.

Grade Medium
Maps N29 St Arnaud, Nelson Lakes Parkmap
Total Walking Time 7–8 hours
Access The alpine township of St Arnaud lies on SH 63. From St Arnaud take the road to the DOC Visitor Centre, and beyond to the carpark at Kerr Bay, where there is a shelter, campsite and toilets. The track finishes on the Mt Robert Road, where during the summer a shuttle pick-up can be arranged. Without transport, it is a further 2 hour walk along the road and through bush tracks back to St Arnaud and Kerr Bay.
Information DOC St Arnaud Tel: 03-521-1806

MARLBOROUGH SOUNDS
MT STOKES • SHIP COVE, QUEEN CHARLOTTE TRACK

MT STOKES

Mt Stokes, the highest point in the Marlborough Sounds, is the only place in the area high enough to support a subalpine habitat. It harbours a curious mix of endemic plants and some not found elsewhere in the South Island. The 1203 metre summit offers one of the finest views in the country, a 360 degree panorama of the Marlborough Sounds including both Pelorus and Queen Charlotte sounds. There is perhaps no better place to visualise the origins of the area: sea-drowned river valleys with the various islands being the tops of partially submerged ridges.

Intriguingly, Mt Stokes lies as close to Wellington's Tararua Range as it does to Marlborough's Richmond Range; both are 50 kilometres distant. The mountain takes its name from Captain John Lort Stokes, who commanded the ship Acheron *during the first comprehensive survey of New Zealand's coastline in the years 1848–1852.*

Okoha Saddle to Mt Stokes 2–2.5 hours

After the tortuous drive from Picton, walkers will be pleased to don boots at Okoha Saddle, where the track begins a steady plod uphill through beech forest. Sadly, a rat plague wiped out a yellowhead (mohua) population that lived in these forests in 2002.

The track continues to ascend steadily up the ridge for a solid 2 hours until the forest thins, reverts to leatherwood, then finally gives way to tussock and alpine plants. The summit is a short distance further on.

In fine weather this is a place to linger and enjoy the outlook. During inclement weather it is, like any mountain-top, a bleak place; walkers need to carry warm clothes and a rain jacket.

Grade Medium
Map Marlborough Sounds Parkmap
Total Walking Time 4–5 hours return
Access From Picton, take Queen Charlotte Drive as far as Linkwater, where you turn off onto Kenepuru Road. At the head of Kenepuru Sound, branch off onto Titirangi Road and follow this as far as Okoha saddle.
Alternative route Walkers can access Mt Stokes by taking a water taxi to Endeavour Inlet, where the Antimony Mines Track provides access to Titirangi Road at a point some 5 km from Okoha Saddle. Despite avoiding most of the driving, this is a much longer approach, and will be beyond all but very fit walkers to complete in a single day.
Information DOC Picton Tel: 03-520-3007

SHIP COVE, QUEEN CHARLOTTE TRACK

The popular Queen Charlotte Track connects Anakiwa with Ship Cove, crossing a mixture of historic and scenic reserves and private land in the Marlborough Sounds. Road and water taxi access allow walkers to enjoy sections of the track without having to embark on its entire 71 kilometre length.

Perhaps the most scenic section, and certainly the one with most historic interest, is that which connects Ship Cove and Endeavour Inlet. Ship Cove was named by the celebrated English mariner Captain James Cook, who spent 100 days here during the 1770s – more time than he spent anywhere else in New Zealand – enjoying the relatively benign climate and sheltered anchorage.

Well defined and marked, the track should not present any problems to walkers of modest fitness. Walkers should be aware that mountain bikers use the track, except during the summer months of December to February.

Ship Cove to Resolution Bay 2–2.5 hours

To start the track arrange water taxi transport to Ship Cove. The cove, known to Maori as Meretoto, became Captain

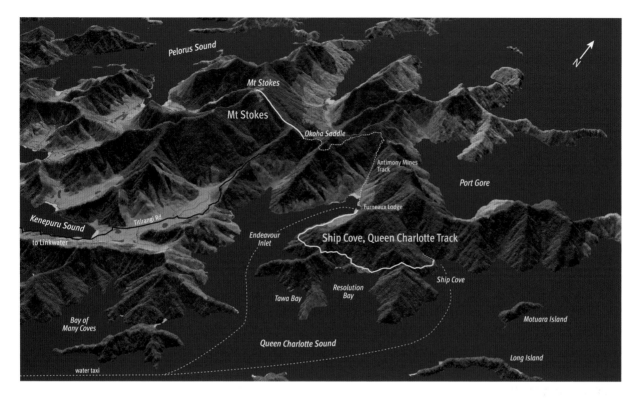

Cook's home away from home during his three New Zealand voyages. Here he made repairs to his ships, rested the crew, and replenished supplies of water and food. The area surrounding the cove is now a Historic Reserve, with an imposing memorial to Cook, information panels and a shelter.

Many walkers choose to first divert up a side track which leads from Ship Cove to an attractive waterfall (90 minutes return). From Ship Cove the Queen Charlotte Track climbs through forest over a ridge then descends to reach Resolution Bay (named after one of Cook's ships), where there is a DOC campsite. Those wanting a shorter walk can arrange a water taxi pick up from here.

Resolution Bay to Furneaux Lodge, Endeavour Inlet 2.5–3 hours
From Resolution Bay the Queen Charlotte Track skirts the shore, then begins a climb over a forested ridge, eventually curling round into Endeavour Inlet – named after another

of Cook's ships. The track gradually descends towards the shoreline to reach Furneaux Lodge, which offers accommodation and café meals. Nearby, a side track leads to another waterfall.

Grade Easy–Medium
Map Marlborough Sounds Parkmap
Total Walking Time 4–5 hours
Access Picton-based water taxis service Ship Cove, Resolution Bay and Furneaux Lodge. **Note**: During extreme fire risk, the track may be closed.
Information DOC Picton Tel: 03-520-3007. The websites www.queencharlottetracknz.com and www.nz.com/travel/queen.charlotte have further information on the track and water taxi operators.

KAIKOURA
KAIKOURA PENINSULA WALKWAY

Not so long ago Kaikoura was a sleepy crayfishing town, but in the last two decades it has reinvented itself as a holiday destination, famous for its whale watching tours. Kaikoura lies at the edge of the deep Hikurangi Trench, where the convergence of warm and cold oceanic currents causes a great upwelling, rich with krill. Although the whales are the best-known of the sea creatures to take advantage of the plentiful feeding available, Kaikoura is also frequented by New Zealand fur seals and a large variety of seabirds – some of which walkers may encounter on this popular coastal walk.

Once an island, the limestone-dominated Kaikoura peninsula was connected to the mainland after river gravels, eroded from the nearby Seaward Kaikoura Range, in-filled the shallow sea that separated it. The range – which has peaks over 2500 metres – shows to advantage from various positions along the track, most noticeably at Point Kean.

In recent years DOC has, in partnership with local iwi, the Kaikoura District Council and Whale Watch Kaikoura, undertaken a grand redevelopment of the track entrances at South Bay and Armers Bay.

Stylised Maori figures depict several of the legends about the peninsula, forming a striking introduction to the walk. Although much of the track connecting the two bays lies on farmland, there is an opportunity to explore the coast on a side track to East Head. The walk will appeal to walkers of all abilities and children will enjoy it too. The first part of the South Bay track to Limestone Bay is also suitable for wheelchairs.

South Bay to Point Kean 60–75 minutes

From the South Bay entrance, past the very stylish waka-shaped toilet block and viewing shelter, the track leads over a new causeway to Limestone Bay. The track has paving stones until the base of the first climb, where it changes to gravel. A brief climb leads up to a viewpoint over South Bay and the coastline south. From here the track wends over flat sheep-grazed farmland, following tall marker poles with a Maori motif. In places, information panels explain the area's natural and human history.

The gravel ends at the junction with the East Head side track (20 minutes return). This leads steeply down to

A walker near a view-point over South Bay

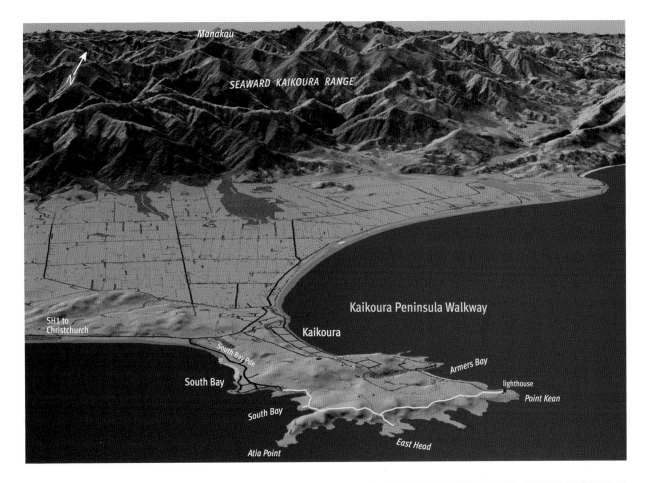

a reef-fringed point, where in summer the South Island's largest breeding colony of red-billed gulls makes a noisy – and smelly – spectacle. Other birds in the area include variable oystercatchers, turnstones and white-faced herons. New Zealand fur seals frequent the point too (keep a safe 10 metres from them, and avoid getting between the animal and the sea).

The main track continues to flank coastal cliffs, wending its way to Point Kean, where a small yellow lighthouse warns ships of the extensive limestone reefs of the peninsula. On a fine day the viewing area has superb views of the Seaward Kaikoura Range. The Armers Bay carpark is 5 minutes away on a paved path, but most walkers will turn back at the point.

Grade Easy

Map 031 Kaikoura

Total Walking Time 2.5–3 hours return (including the side trip to East Head)

Access Just south of Kaikoura township on SH 1, turn off at the sign indicating South Bay. Follow South Bay Parade for 3 km to the large carpark at South Bay where there are toilets, an information panel and viewing shelter.

Alternative route Walkers with less time could walk as far as East Head and return (1.5 hours return)

Information Kaikoura Information Centre Tel: 03-319-5641

ISOLATED HILL SCENIC RESERVE
SAWCUT GORGE

In the Chalk Range of southern Marlborough, rare plants – including the showy purple-flowering Marlborough rock daisy – and strange landforms combine to create a landscape unique in New Zealand. The undoubted highlight of the area is a narrow limestone fissure through which Isolation Creek runs, aptly called Sawcut Gorge.

Slot canyons as narrow as Sawcut Gorge are a rarity in New Zealand, and walkers will get a thrill wandering through its length.

Access to the gorge is from Blue Mountain Station, from which walkers must ask permission to cross private land that leads into the DOC-managed area beyond (the Isolated Hill Scenic Reserve). The route follows the Waima River to its junction with Isolation Creek, with the Sawcut Gorge just upstream of the confluence.

It will suit adventurous walkers of moderate fitness, who must be prepared for multiple river crossings and some route finding. Heavy rain will make the trip impossible, and walkers should set out only on a fair forecast.

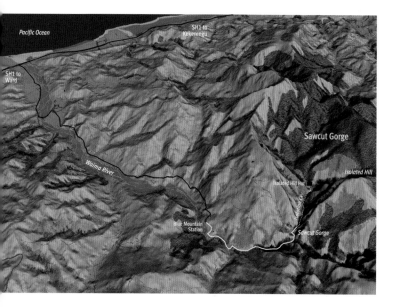

Blue Mountain Station to Sawcut Gorge
1.5–2 hours

From the station, follow farm tracks down to the Waima River, and head upstream, crossing when necessary. Cairns and orange markers indicate the route. After about 40–50 minutes or so, the valley narrows considerably, with high limestone cliffs shading the river. A track on the true left winds up between boulders and shrubby vegetation through a gorge in the Waima, to where the valley opens out again somewhat after a further 40–50 minutes. Keep heading upstream on a marked track on the true right, with one eye out for where Isolation Creek spills in on the left. Sawcut Gorge is about 5 minutes up Isolation Creek, and takes about 5 minutes to walk through. Nowhere more than about 5 metres wide, the gravelly creek has cut through bluffs over 150 metres high and roughly 50 metres long.

Grade Medium–Hard
Maps P29–Q20 Grasmere
Total Walking Time 3–4 hours return
Access From SH 1, 10 km south of Ward, turn off onto Ure Road, and follow it for 12 km (all gravel) to the end at Blue Mountain Station.
Alternative route Walkers wanting a longer trip can continue upstream from Sawcut Gorge to reach Isolated Hill Hut (6 bunks) set on a manuka flat beside a river fork, which would add another 1.5 hours (return) onto the trip.
Information DOC Nelson Visitor Centre Tel: 03-546-9339, Email: nelsonvc@doc.govt.nz

KAHURANGI NATIONAL PARK, WEST COAST
HEAPHY COASTLINE • OPARARA BASIN

HEAPHY COASTLINE

Many trampers who have tackled the entire 82 kilometres of the Heaphy Track remark that they most enjoyed its coastal section. The Heaphy coastline, studded with nikau palms and craggy headlands, and pounded by vigorous West Coast surf, certainly rates as one of the best coastal walks in the country. Walkers can enjoy it over half a day or less. In summer, take repellent for the often-ferocious sandflies.

The track takes its name from explorer and artist Charles Heaphy, who with Thomas Brunner and two Maori guides, Tau and Kehu, walked along this stretch of coastline from Golden Bay in 1846.

Kohaihai Shelter to Scotts Beach 1 hour

From Kohaihai Shelter, the track heads up the Kohaihai Valley for a short distance before crossing a substantial footbridge over the Kohaihai River. A distinctive feature of many rivers on the West Coast, including those on the Heaphy coastline is the tannin stained water, which looks like flowing tea.

Beyond, the track ascends through subtropical forest around Kohaihai Bluff up to a lookout over Scotts Beach some 160 metres above the sea. After a breather here, descend to Scotts Beach. A large triangular granite boulder, lashed by surf and sunk in golden sands, forms a distinctive landmark. Tucked into the forest is a campsite and picnic area.

Scotts Beach to Katipo Creek Shelter 1.5 hours

From the north end of Scotts Beach, energetic walkers may like to walk as far as Katipo Creek, passing Big Rock, Koura and Twin beaches en route. Note that Crayfish Point, which separates the latter two beaches, can be dangerous at high tide. It is prudent to wait for low tide or use the high-tide track.

Grade Easy–Medium
Maps Kahurangi Parkmap, L26 Heaphy
Total Walking Time 5 hours return
Access The track starts at the end of SH 67, some 16 km north of Karamea. At the carpark is the Kohaihai Shelter, picnic tables, information panels and a phone. In summer shuttles service the track.
Information DOC Karamea Tel: 03-782-6652.

The tea-coloured Kohaihai River at the beginning of the Heaphy Track

OPARARA BASIN

The Oparara Basin is a large area of exquisite beech–podocarp forest inland from the West Coast town of Karamea. As well as excellent birdlife, the forest harbours a number of outstanding geological features, including caves, natural bridges and arches.

Several good tracks exist in the basin, centred around the Oparara River; a river that due to natural tannins leaching from the forest and soils has the colour of a dark ale. The smallest but most beautiful of three arches in the area is Moria Gate, a natural limestone bridge which is the remnant of a collapsed cave system. The arch is accessible on a good track, which has recently been extended to connect with Mirror Tarn, a small lake known for its elegant forest reflections. The second and largest arch, the Oparara Arch, is also the result of a collapsed cave system. A third arch at Honeycomb Hill Caves is restricted to a limited number of guided parties.

The tracks are all well-graded and gravelled, and will suit walkers of all abilities and families with school-age children.

Carpark to Moria Gate and Mirror Tarn 1–1.5 hours

Follow the wide, gravelled track through primeval forest for 25–30 minutes to a signposted track junction. Here take the short side track through a narrow cave that leads to the riverside under the arch.

The main track crosses over the top of the arch on a series of concrete paving stones, and around to a viewpoint of the arch. Continuing upstream, the track crosses two tributaries on footbridges, and crests a small rise before reaching the riverbank again. A short distance beyond, a 2 minute side trail leads to Mirror Tarn. From the tarn, the track ends after 15 minutes more walking at the Mirror Tarn carpark. The Moria Gate carpark is 500 metres back along the road.

Carpark to Oparara Arch 40 minutes return

This shorter gravel track leads beside the true right bank of the Oparara River right into the magnificent arch. Vines hang down from the opening, which is 43 metres high, and the Oparara River curls through its tunnel-like 219 metre length.

Above Beech tree, Oparara River
Opposite Oparara Arch

Grade Easy

Maps Kahurangi Parkmap, L27 Karamea.

Total Walking Time 2–2.5 hours for both walks

Access Drive north of Karamea on SH 67 for 10 km until a signpost indicates Oparara Basin (don't take Oparara Road). The 14 km to the carpark is on a winding, narrow, gravel road with some steep sections (allow about 45 minutes driving from Karamea). A toilet is located 1 minute along the Oparara Arch track.

Alternative route Another short 20 minute track leads into two small caves known as the Box Canyon and Crazy Paving Stones (a torch is essential), which are located a further 2.5 km along the Oparara Basin Road.

Information DOC Karamea Tel: 03-782-6652.

PAPAROA NATIONAL PARK, WEST COAST
PORORARI–PUNAKAIKI LOOP

Paparoa National Park became the twelfth in New Zealand when it was established in 1987. The 38,000 hectare park is famous for the Pancake Rocks, a series of stacked limestone formations on the sea edge at Dolomite Point. Limestone is the predominant feature of the coastal part of the park, in contrast to the high granite peaks of the Paparoa Range that form its eastern boundary.

Perhaps the best day walk in the area is a loop track up the Pororari River, and across a connecting track to the Punakaiki River. The Pororari River, flowing gently amongst nikau-studded forest in a valley flanked by the area's distinctive limestone bluffs, is certainly the highlight. The track received a major upgrade in 2006.

Although an undemanding track, the Punakaiki River must be forded once, which may prove impossible after rain. Take plenty of insect repellent for the sandflies.

Pororari River Track 60–75 minutes

A well-graded track follows the true left bank of the river, which is accessible at several points along the track. In

Sculpted limestone on the Pororari River

120

places the emerald green waters of the Pororari have sculpted the limestone beautifully. After about 60–75 minutes, the valley opens out, and the track reaches the junction with the Inland Pack Track (a 2 day tramping trip). A delightful picnic spot can be reached by following this track a short distance left (east) until just before it fords the Pororari River.

Pororari to SH 6 and Punakaiki via Punakaiki River 2–2.5 hours

From the junction, the track begins a climb over the ridge separating the Pororari and Punakaiki rivers. Once across the ridge, the track descends to a ford over the Punakaiki River, which, although not as striking as the Pororari, is nevertheless a distinctive Paparoa canyon. The track fords the river to the south bank to reach the Punakaiki

Valley road, from where it is a 30 minute stroll out to SH 6, and another 30 minutes back to Punakaiki.

Grade Easy–Medium
Map K30 Punakaiki
Total Walking Time 3–3.5 hours (including the walk back along the road to Punakaiki)
Access Punakaiki lies on SH 6 between Greymouth and Westport, and has toilets, cafés, accommodation and a DOC visitor centre. The track starts on the south bank of the Pororari River, 1 km north of the visitor centre, and ends on the Punakaiki Road, 2.5 km from the visitor centre on the south side.
Information DOC Punakaiki Tel: 03-731-1895

WESTPORT
CHARMING CREEK WALKWAY • DENNISTON WALKWAY

Railway line and the Verandah tunnel, Charming Creek Walkway

CHARMING CREEK WALKWAY

The Charming Creek Walkway could be a contender for New Zealand's best walkway, although such judgements are always subjective. Certainly the track offers an impressive amount of interest to walkers: a fascinating history which comes alive through the multitude of relics left in situ, diverse and often magnificent scenery and geology, distinctive flora and fauna – and all this on a gradient that does not exceed 1 in 7.

During the early 1900s, two sawmilling brothers from Granity, Bob and George Watson, came up with an audacious plan to exploit the timber and coal reserves in the upper Ngakawau Valley by building a railway down the fearsome Ngakawau gorge, which in places has sheer sides and a flow often consisting of whitewater churning around immense boulders. Against all odds, the Watson brothers succeeded. The railway ran from 1912 until 1958, when road access through Seddonville made the line redundant.

It is along this largely intact railway line that the Charming Creek Walkway passes; through the gorge, past the tumultuous cascade of the Mangatini Falls, and up into Charming Creek – a tributary that is the Mr Hyde to Ngakawau's Dr Jekyll.

Aptly-named Charming Creek meanders in an unhurried manner, and the silver pine–rimu–beech–manuka forest dominating here contrasts strongly with the dripping, confined rainforest of the Ngakawau.

Although there are several places where parents will have to watch their children, the walkway is suitable for families (but is probably too long for young children if walked both ways).

Walkers should note that mountain bikes are permitted on the track except during the period from 25 December to 25 January and at Easter.

Ngakawau to Watson's Mill 1 hour 15 minutes

From the carpark, the track heads up the valley, following the railway lines for 10 minutes until reaching The Bins, an

area where a siding joined the main Charming Creek railway. From here much of the coal was sent by rail to Westport and shipped to Wellington.

Beyond, the valley narrows, and the Ngakawau River soon begins to thunder. The railway and sleepers remain largely intact, passing through the kinked Irishmans Tunnel, and largely hugging the bank with good views over the river. An endemic daisy *Celmisia morganii* grows here.

Just before Mangatini Falls, the track crosses a substantial footbridge with sublime views. A second tunnel, nicknamed The Verandah, has a wooden boardwalk and rail to aid the walker's passage in the ink-black centre. Beyond,

the track passes under dripping overhangs overlooking the confluence of the Ngakawau River and Charming Creek. Watson's Mill site is a short distance up Charming Creek, where there is a shelter and a toilet.

Watson's Mill to Charming Creek Coal Mine 1 hour 45 minutes

In the much more open valley of Charming Creek the terrain has a completely different atmosphere. The rail lines are largely gone from this section, although sleepers remain in many sections. Listen out for fernbirds and robins, which are common, and the occasional kakariki. Giant land snails of the *Powelliphanta* genus may be observed too.

123

The track crosses Charming Creek and its tributaries several times on wooden bridges, reaching the Mumm's Mill site a further 75 minutes from Watson's Mill.

Here a shed houses an intact restored steam tractor and coal shuttle, with a boiler in another shed nearby. From Mumm's, the track deviates from the old railway line for a significant distance, bypassing a closed tunnel and an old coal-blackened settling pond, to end at the Charming Creek coal mine. Concrete building sides, an old tin shed and a large amount of rusting machinery mark the site, with a nearby wooden bridge completing the track at the end of the Charming Creek Road.

Above *Mangatini Falls, Ngakawau Gorge, Charming Creek Walkway.* **Opposite** *Restored section of brakehead, Denniston Incline*

Grade Easy
Map L28 Mohikinui
Total Walking Time 3 hours each way
Access From Westport drive for 30 km on SH 67 to the township of Ngakawau. The track starts on a signposted side road near the Solid Energy coal processing plant. The far end of the walkway ends at Charming Creek Road, 10 km of gravel road southwest of Seddonville.
Alternative route Walkers wanting a shorter option could walk as far as the Mangatini Falls or Watson's Mill and return.
Information DOC Westport Tel: 03-788-8009

DENNISTON WALKWAY

Set high on a largely treeless, often foggy and frequently windswept plateau on the northern West Coast, Denniston was an unlikely place for up to 1500 people to live.

But for several decades Denniston was the most important coal mine in New Zealand, producing around 13 million tonnes of coal during its 88 year history.

Coal trucks were sent down an incline with a 500 metre vertical drop – the steepest in the world – that was constructed in 1878–79 to exploit the enormous coal measure of the plateau. Ingeniously, gravity powered the operation, with the weighty coal-filled trucks providing ample momentum to pull up empty returning trucks.

In recent years Denniston has enjoyed something of a revival in popularity, thanks to the enormously successful historical novels, Denniston Rose *and* Heart of Coal *by author Jenny Pattrick. Most visitors come by road, but there is a good walking track to the abandoned town: the Denniston Walkway, which starts at Waimangaroa, north of Westport.*

There is something honest and respectful about approaching the town in the same manner as a whole generation of miners and their families – on foot. At first people rode the coal trucks up and down the incline, but four deaths prompted the construction of the bridle track in 1884. It is a decent 540 metre climb over about 5 kilometres of good benched track, with a side trail to a section of the slowly disintegrating incline, disused since 1967. Moderate fitness is required.

Conns Creek Road to Denniston 3 hours

The track begins to climb immediately, passing through regenerating forest, with the occasional viewpoint of the distant incline. After about 30 minutes, a side track exits to the Denniston Road at the One Mile Log carpark. The main track continues to climb, now in mature forest dominated by kamahi and other hardwoods. A few insubstantial creeks are crossed, with a bridge over Conns Creek. After about 2–2.5 hours, a worthwhile side trail branches off steeply down to the incline. This 20 minute return track ends at a fenced-off viewpoint of a reasonably intact section of the incline.

Beyond here the main track begins a series of zigzags and finally emerges at Denniston at an area known as the Brakehead. DOC have undertaken restoration work here,

and there are three coal trucks in superb condition, as well as a reconstructed section of rail tracks. A 3 minute track leads down to a viewpoint over the incline.

Nearby are crumbling concrete structures, an old shed now serving as an excellent information shelter, and some large winch wheels. Follow the road up past a restored aerial cableway to the main site of the town, or explore several tracks that begin from the Brakehead.

Grade Medium
Map K29 Westport
Total Walking Time 5 hours
Access From Westport, drive north on SH 67 for 15 km to Waimangaroa. The signposted Denniston Walkway starts from a small carpark on Conns Creek Road, 1.4 km from the highway.
Alternative route Provided transport can be arranged to Denniston, walkers could simply follow the walkway down to the Conns Creek carpark (2 hours). At Denniston a whole range of walks are possible: Brakehead Walk (40 minutes return), Town Walks (40 minutes return), Coalbrookdale Walk (2 hours each way).
Information DOC Westport Tel: 03-788-8009

VICTORIA FOREST PARK
MURRAY CREEK GOLDFIELDS TRACK

The town of Reefton, like so many on the West Coast, owes its original existence to mining. Reefton's boom times came in the 1870s and 1880s – a decade after the main gold mining period on the West Coast began in the 1860s – and required considerable capital and effort to extract the gold from quartz reefs.

The relic-littered Murray Creek Goldfields Track offers walkers perhaps the best introduction to the area's history. The Murray brothers first discovered gold in the locality as early as 1866, but significant mining did not occur until the 1870s, when some 200 claims were pegged out. The enormous effort required to position the heavy machinery used in quartz mining was quite staggering. For example, the Ajax battery and boiler, the first to operate on the Murray Creek goldfields in 1872, was shipped to

New Zealand from Australia, barged up the Grey River, carried by dray to Blacks Point, winched up steep slopes above Murray Creek, then finally dragged – over a period of 6 weeks – the last 2.4 kilometres to the mine site!

Payable gold finally dwindled by the 1920s, although coal continued to be extracted profitably as late as the 1960s.

Too much concentrated activity occurred in the area to provide a useful historical summary here, so interested readers should seek out a DOC brochure Walks in the Murray Creek Goldfield or Darrell Latham's book The Golden Reefs (see bibliography).

A convenient loop track – suitable for walkers of moderate fitness – begins and ends at Blacks Point (just east of Reefton) and passes, in order, the sites of the Cement Town, Chandlers Open Cast Mine, Murray Creek Gold Mine, Inglewood Mine and Ajax Battery. Mountain bikers are permitted on the section through Cement Town into the Waitahu Valley, but not around the Ajax and Inglewood areas.

Blacks Point to Inglewood Junction via Cement Town 2–2.5 hours

From the carpark at Blacks Point, the track follows an old lorry road through exotic trees that soon lapses into beech forest. The wide, nicely-benched track is interrupted briefly by a set of stairs around a small bluff. After 35 minutes, the track crosses an old bridge to the true left where the signposted Lankey Creek Track and Energetic Mine branches off.

The main track continues up Murray Creek for 5 minutes before coming to the Ajax Battery turnoff (where walkers complete their loop). Another 10-15 minute walk leads to the Cement Town junction, where a 10 minute return side trip leads to the site of the former Cement Town. Slowly regenerating bush, an old seam of coal and a few scattered relics are all that is left to mark the town site, which was obliterated by opencast mining.

Past the Cement Town junction, the main track crosses a new footbridge (with a view of the old bridge) to the true

Ajax Battery site, Murray Creek Goldfields Track

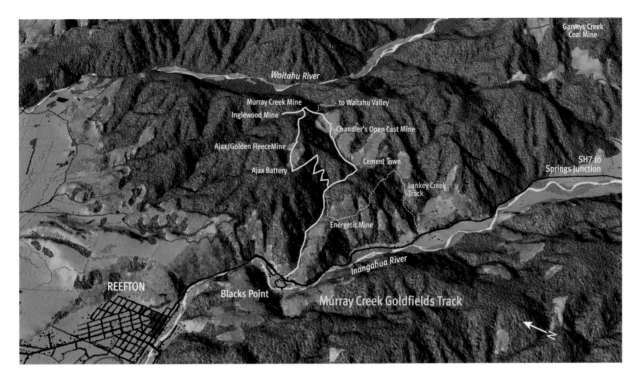

right of Murray Creek. A further 15 minute walk upvalley leads to Chandler's Open Cast Mine, an interesting area of reddish sandstone, with a small artificial pond and relics of more opencast mining. At the Waitahu River Track junction, a further 5 minutes on, head left and begin climbing on a benched track that winds up over slopes forested with pole-beech for 15 minutes to a saddle at the Inglewood Junction.

Inglewood Junction to Blacks Point via Inglewood and Ajax Mines 2–2.5 hours

From the Inglewood Junction it is well worth taking the 40 minute return trip to visit the Inglewood Mine and Battery. Mining here produced limited reward despite strenuous efforts between 1871 and 1912. Among the interesting remains are an old boiler, fluming, winching gear, and a fenced-off mine shaft. So much remains here because it was too costly to retrieve it all from such an isolated location.

Back on the main track, a gentle 20 minute ascent leads through beech forest to the Ajax–Golden Fleece Mine shafts. More relics are encountered at the Ajax Battery site,

10 minutes further on, including parts of a 15-stamper battery, boiler and steam engine. From here the track climbs to cross a low forested saddle, then descends in zigzags for 20 minutes on the Royal Track to intercept the main Murray Creek Track. From there, it is a 40 minute walk back along the track to Blacks Point.

Grade Medium
Map L30 Reefton
Total Walking Time 5 hours (including the 40 minute side trip to Inglewood Mine)
Access Blacks Point is 3 km east of Reefton on SH 7, where there is a carpark, picnic area and the Blacks Point Museum (well worth a visit, but closed in winter). The DOC visitor centre in Reefton has interesting history and information too.
Alternative route Walkers could choose to exit out to SH 7 via the Lankey Creek Track, which would add an additional 1.5–2 hours to the walk.
Information DOC Reefton Tel: 03-732-8391

WESTLAND/TAI POUTINI NATIONAL PARK
ALEX KNOB • HARIHARI COASTAL WALK

ALEX KNOB

Alex Knob is the first significant point on the Fritz Range, the main ridge on the western side of the Franz Josef Glacier. The 1303 metre peak offers incredible views of the glacier and the high peaks rising above the Franz Josef névé, as well as the Tasman Sea and flats of Westland.

The peak is named after Alex Graham (1881–1957), a pioneering guide and West Coast identity, who made a number of fine first ascents in the Southern Alps, including Mt Aspiring, and a grand traverse of Aoraki/Mt Cook. Walkers will earn their views though: this a steep, demanding route involving a 1200 metre ascent which will suit experienced and well equipped trampers only. During winter ice axe and crampons may be necessary. Carry plenty of water, and start early.

Carpark to Lake Wombat 45 minutes

The track as far as Lake Wombat is fairly undemanding, passing through rainforest dominated by rata, rimu, kamahi and Hall's totara. After about 30 minutes, the track reaches the junction with the Lake Wombat track. Here, a 15 minute side track descends into a basin where a boardwalk crosses swampy terrain to reach the small, tranquil lake.

The lake was named after gold miner John Irwin, who had the nickname 'Wombat Jack'. Walkers may spot grey ducks or black shags on the lake.

Lake Wombat turnoff to Alex Knob 3.5 hours

Soon past the track junction the main Alex Knob Track starts a serious climb, zigzagging up through forest with some

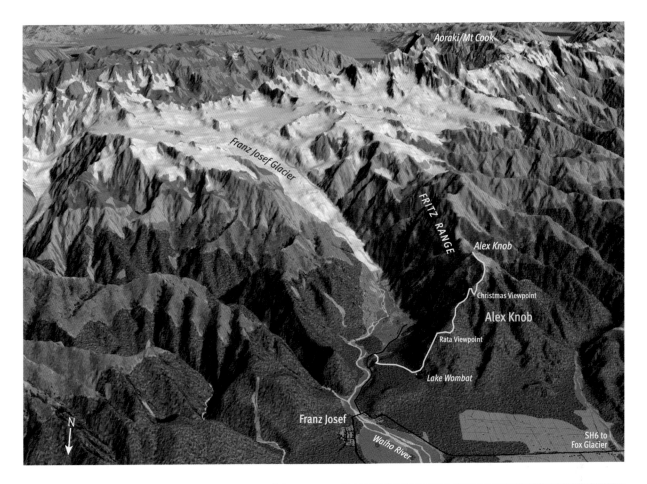

Aoraki/Mt Cook

Franz Josef Glacier

FRITZ RANGE

Alex Knob

Christmas Viewpoint

Alex Knob

Rata Viewpoint

Lake Wombat

Franz Josef

Waiho River

SH6 to
Fox Glacier

N

views of the valley below. After about 400 metres of the ascent, the track reaches the Rata Viewpoint, where the Franz Josef Glacier first comes into sight. Above Rata, the gradient eases somewhat as the track follows the ridge crest, climbing another 400 metres to reach a second viewpoint called Christmas Outlook.

Higher up, walkers will observe the vegetation becoming increasingly stunted as altitude begins to exert its influence. Here *Dracophyllum fiordense*, a type of grass tree normally associated with Fiordland, makes its most northerly occurrence in New Zealand. Finally, above the bushline, snow poles lead across tussock grasslands to the summit, where a plane table indicates the major peaks in view.

Opposite *The upper Franz Josef Glacier névé from Alex Knob*

Grade Hard
Maps G35–H35 Franz Josef
Total Walking Time 7–8 hours return
Access From SH 6 just south of Franz Josef, turn off onto the Glacier Access Road at the Waiho River bridge. Follow the road for 2.5 km until the signposted track start.
Alternative route Lake Wombat makes a shorter destination (grade easy, allow 1.5 hours return), as do the other two lookouts Rata and Christmas (both grade medium, allow 3.5 and 4.5 hours return respectively).
Information DOC Franz Josef Tel: 03-752-0796, Email: franzjosefvc@doc.govt.nz

HARIHARI COASTAL WALK

State Highway 6, which traverses much of the length of the West Coast, is one of the country's most scenic drives. Many motorists find it somewhat surprising, then, that so few sections follow the actual coastline. This walk provides a not-to-be-missed opportunity to experience coastal Westland.

Accessible from the town of Harihari, the well-benched track loops between the Wanganui and Poerua river mouths, traversing luxuriant coastal forest past whitebaiters' baches, and crossing pakihi wetlands to a section of coast where the forest rubs shoulders with the sea.

The coastal section can be safely walked only within 2–3 hours either side of low tide; DOC posts tide tables at the carpark, or they are available in the local newspaper, the West Coast Times.

This is an ideal family walk, with mainly flat, easy walking. It is worth attempting even when rain seems likely: the coast receives far less precipitation than inland areas, where during westerly weather the mountains enforce heavy orographic rainfall.

Road to Mt Oneone and Poerua River Mouth
60–75 minutes

From the carpark the track heads towards the sea, passing a junction (where the loop ends) after 2 minutes. Keep right. Boardwalked sections avoid most of the potentially muddy track. During spring this part of the track is used mostly by whitebaiters accessing their stands on the Wanganui River.

After 30–40 minutes the track emerges onto the estuarine mouth of the Wanganui River, where Mt Oneone (56 m) forms a prominent wedge on the skyline. The hill formed after retreating glaciers deposited moraine some 16,000–18,000 years ago. Follow yellow and blue poles around the estuary shore amongst piles of logs and debris (washed up from the river's frequent spates) to reach the base of Mt Oneone. Unfortunately the unstable nature of the hilltop has forced DOC to close the side-track which leads up to a splendid viewpoint on top. The main track leads out to the coast after another few minutes.

Head south along the shore, on pebble-strewn sands at first, then amongst boulders cast down from the cliffs near the Poerua River mouth. Watch out for the yellow and blue post where the track heads inland.

Sunset over Mt Oneone and Wanganui River mouth, Harihari Coastal Walk, West Coast

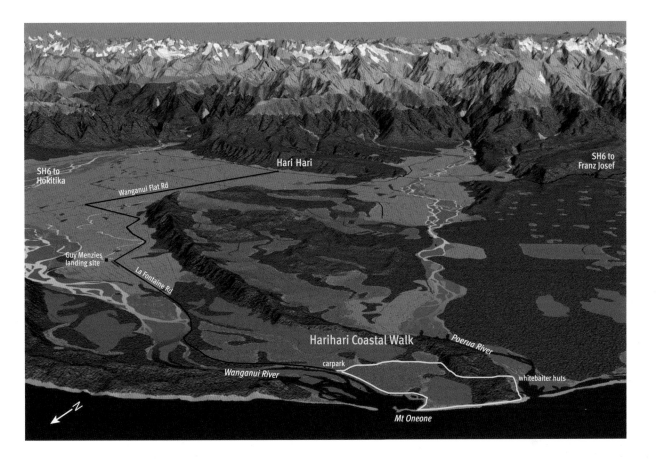

The map shows labels: SH6 to Hokitika, Wanganui Flat Rd, Hari Hari, SH6 to Franz Josef, Guy Menzies landing site, La Fontaine Rd, Harihari Coastal Walk, Poerua River, carpark, whitebaiter huts, Wanganui River, Mt Oneone

Poerua River Mouth and Carpark 1.5 hours

After cresting a small rise, the track descends to near the Poerua River, where some whitebaiters' baches are located. In times past, Maori had summer eeling camps situated here. From the coast, the track cuts across a low rise – another moraine deposit now heavily forested. There's a seat with a view over the pakihi wetland. The track descends to cross an arm of this wetland, and then the Oneone River on a footbridge. Kahikatea, New Zealand's tallest tree, dominates the area, and during the 1930s an industry sprang up to mill the wood, which proved ideal for butter boxes. The last section of track follows a straight section of the old logging tramway used to haul out logs to nearby timber mills. Operations ceased in the late 1950s. The loop concludes 2 minutes before the carpark.

Grade Easy

Maps I34 Harihari

Total Walking Time 2.5–3 hours

Access The walk starts from a carpark on La Fontaine Road, 20 km from Harihari (with the last 8 km gravel). The turnoff from SH 6 (onto Wanganui Flat Road) is signposted, along with the turn onto La Fontaine Road. En route, walkers may like to visit the historic site where Australian pioneer aviator Guy Menzies crash-landed in a swamp after completing the first solo trans-Tasman flight in 1931.

Alternative route The Wanganui River mouth makes a worthwhile trip for those who have less time or meet unfavourable tides (60–80 minutes return).

Information DOC Franz Josef Tel: 03-752-0796

WESTLAND/TAI POUTINI NATIONAL PARK
OKARITO PACK TRACK

South Westland World Heritage Area contains a large portion of the 10 per cent that remains of New Zealand's wetlands, habitats that are increasingly recognised as important for their ecological diversity and their water-sponging ability. Okarito Lagoon and its surrounding wetlands sprawl over a wide flat in Westland/Tai Poutini National Park, and the forests here form a continuous sequence from the sea to the highest peaks of the Southern Alps.

Only two dozen or so people live at the tiny hamlet of Okarito near the lagoon's mouth, and thankfully, this is one place where tourism is as yet subservient to the locals' backwater lifestyle. It retains the sense of an older, less hurried New Zealand.

During the mid 1860s, however, Okarito was a bustling, thriving town of some 1500 residents – at the time the largest on the West Coast – boasting seven pubs, two banks and a bakery. With one of the few navigable river bars on the coast, the international port of Okarito drew people from all over the world, seeking their fortunes in the gold-encrusted sands of the area.

The walk described here follows an old pack track used by miners to reach the Three Mile and Five Mile lagoons, both south of Okarito, and both once rich in goldsands. The pack track was constructed in 1866, a year after gold fever first hit Westland, to avoid a route along the coast which could be treacherous at high tide.

By combining the pack track with the coastal route and making a side trip to Okarito Trig, walkers can complete a satisfying loop. Be aware that the coastal section should be tackled only within 2–3 hours either side of low tide – DOC posts tide tables on the track entrance.

The Strand to Three Mile Lagoon Footbridge via Okarito Pack Track 1.5 hours

From the carpark near the end of The Strand, cross a stile over a fence onto the wide and heavily-gravelled track. This crests a small rise after about 10 minutes where a seat offers views over the sea. After a further 10 minutes the signposted side trip to Okarito Trig branches off. Allow an additional 40 minutes return for this track. A series of wooden steps makes for an honest leg stretch up to the outstanding viewpoint, arguably the finest in South Westland. From the wooden platform walkers can see Okarito Lagoon and township, the vast swathe of dense podocarp–hardwood forest in Westland National Park, as well as a great arc of the Southern Alps stretching from Mt Adams to Aoraki/Mt Cook.

The main track continues through wind-shorn forest, with only a couple of glimpses of the sea. Past Kohuamarua Bluff a gentle descent leads to a seat overlooking the coastline at Three Mile Lagoon. Nearby, a 5 minute side track leads down to a footbridge over the lagoon exit, where there are views almost as good as from the trig. The main track ends on the pebble-speckled coastline near the lagoon mouth.

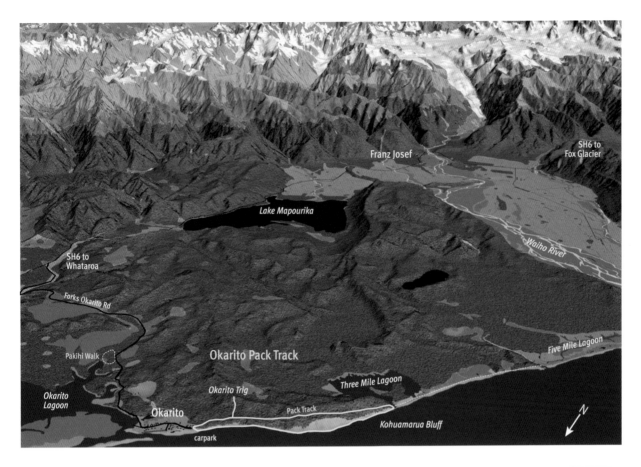

Labels on map: Franz Josef · SH6 to Fox Glacier · Lake Mapourika · Waiho River · SH6 to Whataroa · Forks Okarito Rd · Five Mile Lagoon · Pakihi Walk · Okarito Pack Track · Three Mile Lagoon · Okarito Trig · Okarito Lagoon · Okarito · Pack Track · Kohuamarua Bluff · carpark

Three Mile Lagoon Mouth to Okarito via Coast
1 hour 20 minutes

This section of the walk is much more appealing than the pack track, both for its views and the chance to enjoy a coastal environment. During times when the lagoon exit is not running, it is possible to walk south along the coast as far as Five Mile Lagoon, but most walkers opt to head straight towards Okarito. Both pebbles and sand sink lightly under each footfall, denying walkers the ability to fully stride out, but the compensation is the salty tang of the waves crashing in, the possibility of spotting New Zealand fur seals, and the sea mist lingering in the vegetation of the coastal bluffs. Where the bluffs end, the track heads inland to reach the carpark.

Grade Easy

Maps G35, H35 Franz Josef

Total Walking Time 3–3.5 hours (including Okarito Trig side trip)

Access Okarito is reached on the 11 km sealed Forks Okarito Road, which branches off SH 6 18 km north of Franz Josef. There is a camping ground, various types of accommodation, and a charming YHA hostel in the old schoolhouse. Check out the historic Donovans Store too, one of Westland's oldest buildings.

Information DOC Franz Josef Tel: 03-752-0796

Opposite A boulder at Three Mile Lagoon, Okarito Pack Track

WESTLAND/TAI POUTINI NATIONAL PARK
LAKE MATHESON

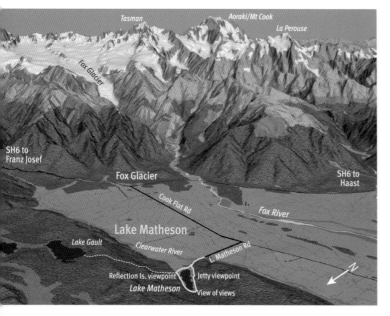

Mts Tasman and Aoraki/Mt Cook reflected in Lake Matheson

Lake Matheson occupies a small, glacier-carved depression on a densely forested flat west of the Southern Alps. On a calm, clear day the lake reflects to perfection New Zealand's two highest peaks, Aoraki/Mt Cook and Mt Tasman. At sunrise or sunset the view can be simply sublime.

An extremely popular, high-grade walk circles the lake, with several viewpoints en route; the best at the far, western, end of the lake is called the View of Views. Walkers of all abilities and families will find this a rewarding walk, and the first part of the track to the jetty viewpoint is negotiable by wheelchairs.

Lake Matheson Track 1.5 hours

Soon after leaving the carpark, the track crosses a footbridge over the Clearwater River. Here the track crosses a slight rise, which is an old moraine ridge now covered with kahikatea and rimu. A few minutes later the track reaches the junction where walkers will complete their loop. Stay left. After about 20 minutes, the track reaches the jetty viewpoint, the first of three. Another 25 minutes walking leads to the View of Views, with Reflection Island 10 minutes further on. At the eastern end of the lake, a side track to Lake Gault branches off, from where it is just a 10 minute walk back to the carpark.

Grade Easy

Maps G35, H35 Franz Josef

Total Walking Time 1.5 hours return

Access From SH 6 at Fox Glacier turn off onto Cook Flat Road, and follow it for 5 km until a signpost indicates a turn right onto the Lake Matheson Road. The carpark is 1 km further on, where there is a café and toilets.

Alternative route Walkers can extend their walk by taking the track to Lake Gault, which climbs 200 metres over a forested ridge to reach the larger but less scenic lake. Allow an additional 2 hours for the walk, which is of tramping track standard.

Information DOC Fox Glacier Tel 03-751-0807, Email: foxglaciervc@doc.govt.nz

LEWIS PASS NATIONAL RESERVE
LAKE DANIELLS

Lake Daniells is one of a number of attractive lakes in the Lewis Pass area formed by landslides. Walkers of moderate fitness can reach the tranquil lake on a gentle, well-graded and well-marked track that passes through stately beech forests, where the birdlife is good. Botanically, the area is of interest due to the presence of all three native beech mistletoes (yellow, red and scarlet). For most of the year these parasitic plants are difficult to identify from their beech tree host, but during spring they flower vibrantly.

Marble Hill Picnic Area to Manson–Nicholls Memorial Hut (24 bunks, wood stove, $10/night)
2.5–3 hours

From the carpark at the Marble Hill Picnic Area, follow the well-graded and gravelled track for 5–10 minutes to The Sluice Box, a narrow marble canyon through which the sizeable Maruia River passes. Cross the footbridge over the river. From here the track follows the true right bank of the Alfred River, passing through tall red beech forest at a kind gradient.

Opposite where Pell Stream, a sizeable tributary, joins the Alfred River, a bench seat offers a place to rest. Further up, the track branches up Frazer Stream and after a kilometre or so begins to climb gently over a forested lip to reach Lake Daniells on its southeastern edge. The Manson–Nicholls Hut is nearby, set just back from the jetty, which makes the perfect spot to appreciate the peacefulness of the bush-surrounded lake.

Grade Medium
Maps L31 Springs Junction, M31 Lewis
Total Walking Time 5–6 hours return
Access Situated 4 km east of Springs Junction on SH 7, the Marble Hill carpark has toilets and facilities for roadside camping and picnicking.
Alternative route The Sluice Box makes a very short, easy return trip of about 15–20 minutes.
Information DOC Reefton Tel: 03-732-8391

Lake Daniells jetty at dawn

LAKE SUMNER FOREST PARK – LEWIS PASS NATIONAL RESERVE, CANTERBURY
NINA HUT • CANNIBAL GORGE • LEWIS PASS TOPS

NINA HUT

When DOC replaced the old Nina Hut in 2002, they made an inspired decision on a new location. The old hut, a small and damp affair on the shady side of the Nina River, with no view, was not the most appealing destination. DOC built the larger replacement on a sunny bush knoll offering a good vista of the mountains surrounding the head of the Nina valley.

In summer this all-weather walk is a pure delight, with dappled light falling through the branches of beech trees, numerous swimming holes in the Nina River, and the pleasant lunch spot of the hut as incentives for your exertions. After a heavy winter snowfall, walkers who don't mind the cold will find a completely different, but equally rewarding experience.

State Highway 7 to Nina Hut (10 bunks, wood stove, $10/night) 3–3.5 hours

From the carpark, the well-marked track leads immediately to a swingbridge across the Lewis River. Once across, flat travel ensues through red beech forest, crossing over old river terraces on the true left of the Nina River. After 30–40 minutes walking the track reaches the Nina River, and hugs the north bank for a further 30–40 minutes. A footbridge crosses the Nina at a small attractive gorge (with good swimming nearby) to where the track continues on the true right bank.

More flat walking ensues until the well-benched track begins a long sidle across forested slopes, with a gradual climb. Water is available where the track crosses a few streams. The new Nina Hut lies in a delightful clearing surrounded by bonsai-like mountain beech, with a moss and *Dracophyllum* understorey.

Grade Medium
Maps M31 Lewis, M32 Boyle
Total Walking Time 6–7 hours return
Access The Nina Valley carpark lies on SH 7 (the Lewis Pass highway), 80 km from Culverden or 30 km from Springs Junction. The track start is opposite Palmer Lodge, a stone New Zealand Deerstalkers Association hut.
Alternative route Walkers wanting a shorter day (2–3 hours return) could find plenty of enjoyment in the section as far as the footbridge across the Nina River.
Information DOC Rangiora Tel: 03-313-0820

Reading the hut book in Nina Hut, Lewis Pass National Reserve

CANNIBAL GORGE

The St James has the distinction of being the longest continuous walkway in the country, carving a semi-circle through the Spenser Mountains and Opera Range. Walkers can gain a taste of the walkway on the Cannibal Gorge section, in the Maruia Valley.

In pre-European times, Maori travelled through the Maruia Valley en route between Nelson–Marlborough and the West Coast or Canterbury. Cannibal Gorge earned its nickname 'Kopi-o-Kai-Tangata' or literally 'the gorge where human flesh was eaten' during a clash between rival iwi in the 1800s. Ngati Wharangi, fleeing a strong Ngai Tahu force, who had chased them from the Ahaura and Mawhera (Grey) Valleys, were at last overcome in Cannibal Gorge, and there – in the traditions of the time – killed and eaten by their opponents.

Aside from its interesting history, Cannibal Gorge offers walkers fine beech forests, good views, and all-weather access, as footbridges span all the major streams.

State Highway 7 to Cannibal Gorge Footbridge
30–40 minutes

The well-signposted St James Walkway begins from a carpark near Lewis Pass. A moss-fringed tarn (with a shelter and toilets nearby) offers good views, looking towards the Spenser Mountains. The wide and well-benched walkway passes through a section of stunted, lichen-covered beech

An alpine tarn near the start of the St James Walkway

forest before beginning a descent towards the Maruia Valley. After crossing a couple of small streams, the track sidles to a substantial footbridge over the right branch of the Maruia River. A plaque here explains the area's history.

Footbridge to Cannibal Gorge Hut (20 bunks, wood stove, $10/night) 2.5–3 hours

Once across, the walkway begins an undulating sidle upvalley, weaving in and out of numerous guts. In winter, a few sections of the track are prone to avalanche (these are well marked). At Phil's Knob a lookout offers a view over the valley and across to the Zampa tops. The valley finally opens out again just before Cannibal Gorge Hut, which occupies a grassy river terrace beneath the high ramparts of the Freyberg Range.

Grade Medium
Map M31 Lewis
Total Walking Time 6–7 hours return
Access The carpark for the St James Walkway lies on SH 7 (the Lewis Pass highway), 90 km from Culverden or 20 km from Springs Junction.
Alternative route For family groups or walkers with less time, the stroll as far as the footbridge at Cannibal Gorge proves to be a rewarding walk (allow 1–1.5 hours return). There is also a small loop walk near the start of the St James Walkway amongst lichen-laden beech trees.
Information DOC Rangiora Tel: 03-313-0820

LEWIS PASS TOPS

Lewis Pass is a great meeting place of various parks and reserves: Lake Sumner Forest Park, Nelson Lakes National Park, Victoria Forest Park, Lewis Pass National Reserve and Lewis Pass Scenic Reserve all share boundaries in the area. Neat beech forests, looking almost manicured, form a trademark of the region, as do modest but craggy mountains.

This relatively little-used track is perhaps one of the most underrated in the country. It offers easy access to delightful, tarn-strewn tops with extensive views of the surrounding mountains. As the track begins at 900 metres, the climb to the bushline at 1300 metres proves steep but short.

State Highway 7 to Lewis Pass Tops 1.5–2 hours

Immediately after entering the silver beech forest, the track begins climbing, sharing part of a short 30 minute lookout loop track for the first 100 metres of the ascent. A wooden seat offers the weary a place for a decent breather en route. Silver beech gives way to mountain beech, which becomes stunted, then dwindles until the first of the tussocks appear. The ridge beyond is marked with poles only as far as the first knoll. Before departing further along the tops, take note of the route back.

On the ridge crest walkers find themselves straddling the crest of the Southern Alps, astride both Westland (Lewis Pass National Reserve) and Canterbury (Lake Sumner Forest Park). Alpine flowers abound in summer. Those with time can – in good weather – wander many pleasant kilometres across the undulating tops, past any number of exquisite tarns. Mountains span every horizon, with Mt Technical (1870 m) – a commanding peak with sharp ridges – especially drawing the eye.

Grade Medium–Hard
Map M31 Lewis
Total Walking Time 4–5 hours return
Access Take SH 7 (the Lewis Pass highway), 90 km from Culverden or 20 km from Springs Junction. The track starts from a rough road right at the Lewis Pass summit. Just west of the pass is an inconspicuous carpark (not to be confused with the much larger St James Walkway carpark 1 km east of the pass).
Information DOC Rangiora Tel 03-313-0820

A tarn on the Lewis Pass Tops with Mt Technical beyond

PORT HILLS, CANTERBURY
SIGN OF THE PACKHORSE

Conservationist Harry Ell was a visionary city councillor who promoted preservation of the appealing tussock landscapes of the Port Hills above Christchurch. Early in the 20th century Ell dreamed of a 'Summit Road' stretching across Banks Peninsula from Christchurch to Akaroa, with a series of 15 resthouses and teahouses en route. While his vision proved too ambitious – and expensive – to fully realise, Ell's legendary energy and drive ensured four fine stone buildings were completed: the Sign of the Takahe, the Sign of the Kiwi, the Sign of the Bellbird, and the Sign of the Packhorse.

While the first three (a restaurant, a teahouse, and a shelter) are accessible by road, the Sign of the Packhorse is now a hut lying on the Summit Road Walkway, a section of Ell's road that was never completed. Constructed in 1916–17, the stone hut is an appealing destination with grand views over Lyttelton Harbour, Banks Peninsula and even the distant Southern Alps.

Note there is no access during lambing season (August to the end of Labour weekend in October).

Gebbies Pass to Packhorse Hut (8 bunks, wood stove, $5/night) 1.5–2 hours

From the road end, follow an old farm track, marked by white poles, leading through a mixture of farmland, and later pine forest. Finally, beyond the last of the pines, it emerges onto the open tussock grasslands of Kaituna Pass, lying between Mt Bradley and the Remarkable Dykes. The Department of Lands & Survey restored the Sign of the Packhorse Hut in 1973, with more recent work done by DOC. Those with energy to burn might like to scramble up the steep slopes of Mt Bradley (855 m), a 400 metre climb above the hut (allow 1.5-2 hours return). Mt Bradley has fine views of Banks Peninsula and Mt Herbert, the area's highest peak.

Tramper overlooking the head of Lyttelton Harbour at dawn

Grade Easy
Map M36 Lincoln
Total Walking Time 3–4 hours return
Access From Christchurch drive to the suburb of Cashmere and up Dyers Pass Road. At the Sign of the Kiwi, turn right onto the Summit Road, and follow it till the intersection with Gebbies Pass Road. The track to the Sign of the Packhorse begins up a short side road from here, ending in locked gates.

Alternative route Walkers can choose a different approach to the Sign of the Packhorse using a track beginning from a side road off Kaituna Valley Road (reached on SH 75). Allow 3–4 hours return.
Information DOC Christchurch Tel: 03-379-9758

ARTHUR'S PASS NATIONAL PARK
AVALANCHE PEAK • OTIRA VALLEY • BEALEY SPUR & HUT

AVALANCHE PEAK

In good weather Avalanche Peak offers a superb vantage point to view the mountains surrounding the Arthur's Pass highway. Walkers will appreciate the opportunity to admire Mt Rolleston, one of the park's premier climbing peaks, from close quarters.

On a good summer day the walk is strenuous and requires a head for heights, but otherwise is not overly difficult. In bad weather, however, it is very exposed and should be avoided. During winter, walkers will need alpine skills and equipment – ice axe and crampons. As its name suggests, the peak can be prone to avalanches so check conditions at the Arthur's Pass visitor centre before you leave.

DOC Visitor Centre to Bushline via Avalanche Peak Track 1.5–2 hours

Two tracks lead through mountain beech forest onto the lower flanks of Avalanche Peak. The most accessible is the Avalanche Peak Track which rises steeply and directly behind the visitor centre. It entails a 1000 metre climb, and in places walkers will need to haul themselves up a lattice-work of tree roots lining the track. En route the track passes close to some waterfalls in Avalanche Creek.

Bushline to Avalanche Peak Summit 1.5–2 hours

Once above the bushline, a poled route leads up a prominent spur, across a tussock basin, then climbs a steepish face to join Scotts Track about 500 metres northeast of Avalanche Peak's summit. The ridge narrows as you approach the rocky summit (1833 m). Mt Rolleston rears prominently to the north, barely 4 kilometres away. For a round trip, walkers can descend Scotts Track, which is slightly longer, but gentler on the knees. It ends 1 kilometre north of the visitor centre.

Opposite *A winter view of Mt Rolleston from Avalanche Peak in winter*

Grade Hard
Maps K33 Otira, Arthur's Pass Parkmap
Total Walking Time 6–8 hours return
Access The alpine township of Arthur's Pass lies on SH 73. The track begins from the carpark at the DOC Visitor Centre in the centre of Arthur's Pass village.
Alternative route Fit and experienced walkers can traverse the tops from Avalanche Peak, past Lyell Peak to Mt Bealey, then down a spur which joins a bush track back to the village. This is an unmarked route requiring good navigational skills and a fine, clear day.
Information DOC Arthur's Pass Tel: 03-318-9211

OTIRA VALLEY

Of all the valleys in Arthur's Pass National Park, the Otira is arguably the most enchanting. A place of babbling streams, artfully-strewn rocks and abundant alpine flora, the valley appeals as much for its more subtle details as for the grand mountains which rise on either side.

Another large part of its charm is the accessibility of entering an enclosed alpine environment with a minimum of effort and climbing. The valley is best visited in early summer, when the alpine flowers are most showy. Walkers with a botanical bent will observe, amongst others, giant mountain buttercups, South Island edelweiss, and several species of Celmisia daisies.

Near the valley head, both the Otira face of Mt Rolleston and nearby Mt Philistine rear impressively. In winter the valley can be prone to avalanches so check conditions at the Arthur's Pass visitor centre before you leave.

Carpark to Otira Valley Head 1.5–2 hours

The track starts gently, and the Dobson Nature Walk branches off after a couple of minutes walking. Past the track junction, the well graded Otira Valley track sidles across rocky slopes, amongst tussocks and subalpine shrubs. After about an hour the track reaches a footbridge over the Otira River. Once across, the track dissolves into a cairn-marked route,

with more difficult, rocky terrain underfoot, following the true left bank of the river. This route peters out altogether after about another hour. Energy levels and the weather will dictate when walkers decide to turn around and head back.

Grade Easy
Maps K33 Otira, Arthur's Pass Parkmap
Total Walking Time 2–3 hours return
Access The Otira valley is accessible from a carpark off SH 73, about 6 km north of Arthur's Pass village and about 1 km from the pass summit itself.
Information DOC Arthur's Pass Tel: 03-318-9211

BEALEY SPUR AND HUT

Walkers might be surprised to learn that, in the early 20th century, sheep grazed the tops above Bealey Spur. Bealey Spur Hut was built in 1925 to serve as a shelter during musters. Beech pole framing is an interesting feature of this rustic building, now recognised as one of several important historic sites in Arthur's Pass National Park.

The hut is accessible on a pleasant, rarely strenuous track through beech and manuka forest and open areas of tussock on Bealey Spur. This is a good walk for families with school-age children. Lying east of the main divide, partially in the rainshadow of the Southern Alps, Bealey enjoys sunnier weather than Arthur's Pass, and a nearby pub offers a watering hole for the end of the day. The pub, last in a long line of hotels that has occupied the site since 1860s, has a family-friendly atmosphere and children will enjoy the several moa statues in the grounds.

Bealey to Bealey Spur Hut (6 bunks, $5/night) 2–3 hours

The track begins gently enough, climbing gradually through very open beech forest. During summer, watch out for mistletoe in flower. After about an hour, the beech thins and the track emerges onto the open face of Bealey (920 m). These open areas are artificial: still unforested after the fires of the grazing era. The track passes through more

Giant Mountain Buttercup, Ranunculus lyallii, Otira Valley

Fine views on the ridge above Bealey Spur Hut.

patches of forest, past a sizeable tarn, then onto a slightly less broad section of the spur. Broad views unfold of the mountains and valleys of the Waimakariri catchment. After passing through a final section of forest, the track reaches the hut. Altogether the track entails a 450 metre ascent over 6 kilometres to the hut. Higher up on Hut Spur the outlook proves even better.

Grade Medium
Maps K34 Wilberforce, Arthur's Pass Parkmap
Total Walking Time 4–6 hours return
Access Bealey is a small bach community lying just off SH 73, some 10 km from Arthur's Pass Village. Turn off the highway onto Cloudesley Road and drive to the carpark at the end of the baches.
Information DOC Arthur's Pass Tel: 03-318-9211

CANTERBURY
MT SOMERS

Many of the country's best viewpoints lie not atop major peaks or mountain ranges, but some distance aside from them. Mt Somers (1687 m), a modest peak in Canterbury's foothills, is such a place. The mountain offers expansive views of the Southern Alps stretching from Mt D'Archiac in the south to the Arrowsmith Range in the north, a panorama perhaps not bettered in Canterbury. In addition, Mt Somer's position well east of the main divide often provides reasonable weather when a westerly or nor'wester soaks other South Island mountain areas. Encircling the mountain is the 2–3 day Mount Somers Walkway, a section of which walkers can use to access the summit of the mountain. While in summer this a straightforward walk, in winter alpine skills and equipment may be needed.

Those with a geological bent will observe the mountain's distinctive rocks, primarily rhyolite and andesite, which provide clues to its volcanic origins. The poor and boggy soil derived from these rocks has encouraged a distinctive alpine plant community to develop on the mountain.

Sharplin Falls Carpark to Staveley Hill 2 hours

Behind the shelter at the carpark, take the signposted track to Staveley Hill (1085 m) and Mt Somers. This is part of the Mount Somers Walkway. Through beech forest the track begins climbing immediately to Hookey Knob, where the ascent eases for a short section. More climbing ensues along a ridge, with the beech forest becoming more stunted, and finally giving way to subalpine shrubs around Staveley Hill.

Walkers beside a tarn on the western slopes of Mt Somers

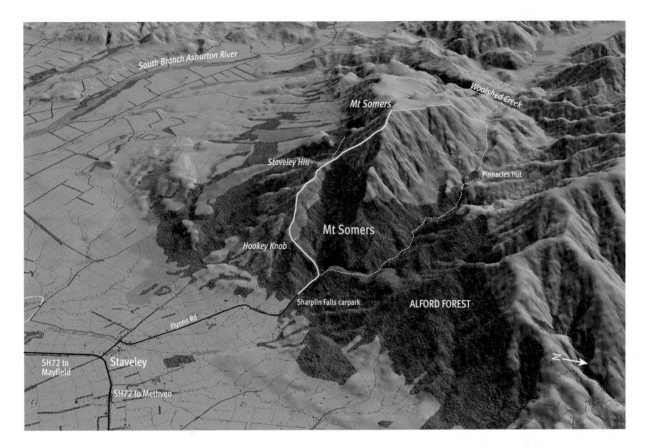

Staveley Hill to Mt Somers Summit 1.5–2 hours

About 10 minutes walk past Staveley Hill, take a poled route that branches off the main Mt Somers Walkway. Follow the poles up through subalpine shrubs for a short distance before the terrain becomes rocky and exposed. Steep, stony travel ensues up to a prominent ridge that curls onto the mountain summit.

A permanent stone cairn, cemented in place, and surrounded by a circular wooden structure, marks the broad, flat-topped summit. On a clear day, a great swathe of the central Southern Alps is visible. Lake Heron lies in the middle distance, and Winterslow is the main summit on the nearest range to the north. Eastwards, laid out like a quilt, are the Canterbury Plains.

Grade Hard

Maps K36 Methven

Total Walking Time 6–8 hours return

Access At Staveley, a small village on SH 72 turn off onto Flynns Road. At the road end there is the Sharplin Falls carpark, which has a shelter and toilets.

Alternative route Fit and experienced walkers may like to tackle the following round trip. From Flynn's Road take the Mt Somers Walkway to Pinnacles Hut, and on to the saddle before Woolshed Creek. Beyond the saddle, the route to Mt Somers is completely unmarked, and navigation skills are essential. Above the saddle, climb moderately steep slopes until gaining a flat plateau northwest of Mt Somers, then follow the broad ridge southeast to Mt Somers. Descend on the route described above.

Information DOC Christchurch Tel 03-379-9758

AORAKI/MOUNT COOK NATIONAL PARK
SEALY TARNS • HOOKER VALLEY

SEALY TARNS

The two attractive small lakes known as Sealy Tarns occupy a tussock ledge high above Mount Cook Village. A lookout beside the tarns offers outstanding views over the Hooker Valley with the great pyramid of Aoraki/Mt Cook shouldering into the sky above it. Further east the Tasman Valley and Liebig Range are prominent. While the track's steepness (involving a 500 metre ascent) deters some walkers, it is still a very popular destination.

Sealy Tarns are accessed from the Whitehorse Hill carpark. Walkers without their own transport can reach Whitehorse Hill on the Kea Point Track, which begins at Mount Cook Village. Allow an extra 1–1.5 hours return.

Whitehorse Hill to Sealy Tarns 1.5–2 hours

A flat section of wide, gravelled track leads from the carpark towards the Sealy Range. After 5 minutes walk the track joins the Kea Point Track, and bends northwards with Mt Sefton prominent ahead. The turnoff to the Sealy Tarns Track is signposted a further 10 minutes along. In a series of steps, benched by old railway sleepers, the track ascends rapidly in a manner that stretches both legs and lungs. Subalpine shrubs surround the track at first, but higher up the terrain becomes rocky, with tussock and alpine herbs the dominant vegetation. With each step the views unfold further.

The steepness of track rarely eases until the track crests a prominent tussock ledge. Nearby lie Sealy Tarns and their famous reflections. From the wooden seat beside the tarns, walkers can consider the complexity and origins of the surrounding landforms. New Zealand's highest mountain range, the Mount Cook Range, rises in a series of increasingly high peaks, culminating in Aoraki itself. Below, where the Hooker and Mueller glaciers merge, the barren, moraine-covered landscape and growing terminal lakes bear testimony to glacial retreat. Eastwards, the flats of Tasman River valley provide contrast to the surrounding terrain, buckled and tilted by the process of plate tectonics.

Grade Medium
Maps H36 Mount Cook, Aoraki/Mount Cook Parkmap
Total Walking Time 3–4 hours return
Access Mount Cook Village is reached on SH 80, which branches off SH 8 near Twizel. Shortly before reaching the village, turn off up the Hooker Valley Road. At the road end is the Whitehorse Hill camping area, with toilets, a shelter and picnic area.
Alternative route Very fit and well-equipped walkers can continue upwards past the tarns to the Sealy Range and Mueller Hut. This is a full day on exposed alpine tops following a poled route, and can be prone to avalanches.
Information DOC Mt Cook Tel: 03-435-1186

HOOKER VALLEY

The Hooker Valley track is undoubtedly amongst the best alpine walks in New Zealand. The easy, well-benched track leads walkers beneath the highest peaks of the Southern Alps, including Aoraki/Mt Cook and Mt Sefton, amongst a profusion of alpine plants, to reach the austere environment of the Hooker Glacier terminal lake. Suitable for walkers of all abilities, and ideal for those with young children, this is a place where both majestic peaks and delicate flora offer beauty on two vastly different scales. Late spring and early summer (late November to January) are when the alpine plants flower most profusely.

Whitehorse Hill to Hooker Glacier Terminal Lakes 1.5 hours

The wide, gravelled track departs Whitehorse Hill and heads towards the Hooker River. A short side track leads to a pyramid-like memorial to climbers and others who have died in the park. Beyond, the track passes a good viewpoint over the Mueller Glacier terminal lake: a place of teetering moraines with the imposing backdrop of Mt Sefton's ice-cliffs.

After 20 minutes walkers reach a large footbridge spanning the churning Hooker River. Across the far side the narrower track is carved out of steep rock cliffs. Barriers ensure safe access for children. A further 20 minute walk around a series of stairs and ledges leads to a second large footbridge crossing back to the true right of the Hooker River. The terrain opens up, with the track passing through a meadow of alpine plants, and suddenly Aoraki/Mt Cook rears into breathtaking view.

At a footbridge over Stocking Stream is a small shelter. Beyond, flat travel leads to the stony shores of the Hooker Glacier terminal lake. Sizeable chunks of ice, calved from the gritty glacier front, often float in the lake.

Grade Easy

Maps H36 Mount Cook, Aoraki/Mount Cook Parkmap

Total Walking Time 2.5–3 hours return

Access Mount Cook Village is reached on SH 80, which branches off SH 8 near Twizel. Shortly before reaching the village, turn off up the Hooker Valley Road. At the road end is the Whitehorse Hill camping area, with toilets, a shelter and picnic area.

Alternative route Walkers without their own transport can reach Whitehorse Hill on the Kea Point Track which begins at Mount Cook Village. Allow an extra 1–1.5 hours return.

Information DOC Mt Cook Tel: 03-435-1186

KANUKA SCENIC RESERVE, DUNSTAN MOUNTAINS, CENTRAL OTAGO
KANUKA TRACK

The recently developed Kanuka Track offers a rare opportunity for a half-day walk in one of Central Otago's distinctive block mountain ranges. The 10 kilometre walk begins and ends at Logantown, an historic mining site north of Cromwell. Marked by orange-sleeved poles, the track loops around the lower slopes of the Dunstan Mountains, passing through open kanuka forest, across several gullies, and around the schist tors for which Central Otago is justly famed. There are good views of Lake Dunstan, the Pisa Range and the Clutha Valley en route.

While this is by no means a beautiful or wholly natural landscape – indeed parts are highly modified, with sheep and rabbits still present – it is certainly an intriguing one.

An added bonus is the chance to return to your vehicle via the historic Matilda Battery site and the wonderful stone hut remains of Welshtown. Along with Logantown, the latter two areas are part of the Bendigo Historic Reserve, which in turn is under the umbrella of the Otago Goldfields Park. Indeed, walkers who do not have time for the Kanuka Track could easily enjoy a couple of hours exploring the old mining towns.

Take plenty of water as there is none en route, and in summer you'll need good sun protection.

Logantown to Torumano 2.5–3 hours

For the first 200 metres the track is benched, passing stone wall remains until meeting the Matilda Battery Track, where the Kanuka Track branches off. The track initially sidles through patches of briar and kanuka before following an old vehicle track across flat terrain for 20–30 minutes to reach the edge of School Creek, just past a stile over a fence. Here the dramatic rocky nature of the range becomes more apparent. The descent into School Creek is the first of many sidles into and out of gullies, with the track gradually climbing towards the crest of the nearby range. Open places offer good westward views of the Pisa Range and Clutha Valley.

The track reaches a large fence marking private land near an area of impressive tors at Torumano, then sidles across slopes towards a knoll to the north. Here, between more tors, the startling blue of Lake Dunstan first comes into view. There are plenty of schist overhangs to seek either shade or respite from the wind.

Torumano to Matilda Track Junction 1.5–2 hours

A descent from the knoll leads down a brow over Pt 588 m that ends in Chinamans Creek. Poles lead upvalley through willow and poplars to reach a stone hut ruin, which speaks of cold winters and lonely exile. Nearby is a rock overhang with some rusting mining relics in situ. The track crests a small rise, descends to follow a fenceline for a short distance, then climbs again through kanuka to intercept the inward track above the School Creek gully. Follow the track back to the Matilda Track Junction.

Junction to Logantown via Matilda Battery Track and Welshtown 45–60 minutes

However tired you are from your exertions on the Kanuka Track, this short additional track is not to be missed. The walk, marked by yellow-topped wooden posts, leads immediately to the site of the Matilda Battery, which once boasted 20 stampers. Stone walls, hut remains and a chimney feature prominently in what was an industrious place during the years 1878–84. Several deep shafts in the area are blocked off with iron grates, but beware of many others which are unmarked and unfenced. From the Matilda Battery site the track forks; either route leads to Welshtown, which is situated on a ridge a short climb ahead. The stone hut remains here must be amongst the best preserved in Otago, and remain steadfast against the winds that blow the surrounding tussocks. Perhaps the most photogenic are those at the former Pengally's Hotel, just across a gully with a small wetland. Return to Logantown via the road.

Grade Medium
Map G41 Cromwell (note the Kanuka Track is unmarked on the map)
Total Walking Time 5–6 hours return
Access From Cromwell drive north on SH 8 for 16 km to Crippletown. Here turn off on the gravel Bendigo (or Loop) Road and drive for 3.5 km to Bendigo, where there is an information panel explaining the area's history. Turn right and drive up a steep dirt road for 3 km to Logantown. Park here and walk back along the road 200 metres to the signposted track start. Alternative parking is available at Welshtown, where there is a toilet and another information panel.
Alternative route From Welshtown an alternative route back to Logantown follows the Aurora Track, which will take an extra 45–60 minutes.
Information DOC Wanaka Tel: 03-443-7660
Email: wanakavc@doc.govt.nz

WEST MATUKITUKI VALLEY, MOUNT ASPIRING NATIONAL PARK
ASPIRING HUT • ROB ROY GLACIER

ASPIRING HUT

The Matukituki Valley, a classic U-shaped glacial valley set amongst grand peaks, is the gateway to Mt Aspiring/Tititea and the historic Aspiring Hut. The well-formed and easy track crosses a sheep- and cattle-grazed pastoral lease on the valley floor to reach the Mount Aspiring National Park boundary near Aspiring Hut. The hut offers expansive views of Mt Aspiring (3033 m), a spearhead of a mountain that many observers have called the Matterhorn of the south.

Although a decent length (some 18 kilometres return), the track is not taxing and the terrain proves easy enough to keep your hands in your pockets and your eyes on the peaks. It's a deservedly popular walk.

Raspberry Flat to Aspiring Hut (38 bunks, wood burner) 2–3 hours

From the Raspberry Flat carpark, the West Matukituki Track crosses open farm country on a farm vehicle track on the true right. After 20–25 minutes, the Rob Roy Track branches off over a footbridge.

Carry on up the valley across more flats and past some stockyards, to where the track climbs around slopes well above the river. Brides Veil Stream cascades off Shotover Saddle above. After descending to more flats, the track passes the locked Cascade Hut with the valley curving northwards. More flats lead to the appealing stone-clad Aspiring Hut, built between 1944 and 1949 by the New Zealand Alpine Club in a position aimed to maximise views of its namesake peak.

Mt Aspiring was first climbed in 1909 by guides Jack Clarke and Alex Graham with Major Bernard Head, using the west face and northwest ridge, on the left-hand skyline. The steeper southwest ridge, in the centre of the view, was not climbed until 1936.

Grade Medium
Maps E39 Aspiring, F39 Matukituki, Mount Aspiring Parkmap
Total Walking Time 4–6 hours return
Access From Wanaka, take the Wanaka–Mount Aspiring Road along the southern shores of Lake Wanaka and up the Matukituki Valley. The first 21 km of the 51 km drive is sealed, and the last 30 km has several fords which can be impassable after heavy rain or snowmelt. Allow a good hours drive. At the Raspberry Flat carpark, there is a shelter, information and toilets. During summer shuttles service the area.
Alternative route Another worthwhile walk in the area is the Glacier Burn, in the East Matukituki Valley (4 hours return). This requires fording the river.
Information DOC Wanaka Tel: 03-443-7660
Email: wanakavc@doc.govt.nz

ROB ROY GLACIER

Rob Roy is one of the more significant peaks in the Matukituki Valley, with an impressive glacier spilling off its eastern flanks. This outstanding day tramp follows a track up the Rob Roy Stream, climbing to an alpine basin above the bushline which offers fine views of the glacier, overhanging formidable bluffs in the upper valley. The glacier is a retreating remnant of a much larger glacier that carved out the Matukituki Valley and its tributaries during the last ice age.

The Rob Roy walk branches off the West Matukituki Track, the same as that used to access Aspiring Hut. As well as the spectacular scenery, walkers are likely to encounter kea in the vicinity. It suits walkers of moderate fitness.

Raspberry Flat to Rob Roy Stream Bushline 2–2.5 hours

From the Raspberry Flat carpark, the West Matukituki Track crosses open farm country on a farm vehicle track on the true right. After 20–25 minutes, a signpost indicates the start of the Rob Roy Track. After crossing the West Matukituki

River on a footbridge, the track enters beech forest and fol-
~~~~~~~~~~~ ~~~ ~~nk for 20 minutes up to a bench seat

and Homestead Peaks. During winter, ~~~~~
down black bluffs.

Grade Medium

Maps E39 Aspiring, F39 Matukituki, Mount Aspiring Parkmap

Total Walking Time 4 hours return

Access From Wanaka, take the Wanaka–Mount Aspiring Road
along the southern shores of Lake Wanaka and up the Matukituki Valley. The first 21 km of the 51 km drive is sealed,
and the last 30 km has several fords which can be impassable
after heavy rain or snowmelt. Allow a good hours drive. At
the Raspberry Flat carpark, there is a shelter, information and
toilets. During summer shuttles service the area.

Alternative route Experienced trampers can explore the
valley head beyond where the track finishes, but should be
wary of avalanche danger during spring and winter.

Information DOC Wanaka Tel: 03-443-7660
Email: wanakavc@doc.govt.nz

Prezado Clienete,

Sentimos muito pelo extravio de sua bagaem. Tenha certeza de que estamos implementando todos os esforços para localizar seus pertences e devolvê-los o mais breve possível.

A fim de amenizar este inconveniente, gostaríamos de oferecer este "kit com alguns itens para o seu conforto.

Szanowni Państwo,
Serdecznie przepraszamy za niedogodności.
Zapewniamy, że dokładamy wszelkich starań, aby odnaleźć bagaż i dostarczyć go Państwu jak najszybciej. Prosimy o przyjęcie zestawu podstawowych artykułów toaletowych. Mamy nadzieję, że okaze się Państwu przydatny.

ทางการบินขออภัยในความไม่สะดวก เป็นอย่างยิ่ง และขอรับรองว่า ในขณะนี้เรากำลัง ดำเนินการทุกวิถีทางเพื่อนำกระเป๋าสัมภาระ ของท่านกลับคืนมาให้เร็วที่สุดเท่าที่จะทำได้

THE STACK CONSERVATION AREA, WANAKA
ROYS PEAK

Roys Peak (1578 m) is a significant summit close to Wanaka offering superlative views of the nearby lake, Mt Aspiring, and a whole host of other mountains. Although the walk largely follows a farm vehicle track, this is a steep, demanding route involving a 1200 metre climb, and the tops are very exposed. On a fine day however, the increasingly good views provide incentive to keep plodding upwards, and the walk is popular.

Although the route is obvious, it is unmarked and could be obscured by heavy winter snow. During winter, walkers will probably need to add crampons and ice axe to their kit, and whatever the weather be sure to carry plenty of water and warm clothing.

Note that the first half of the track crosses private farmland, with sheep and cattle present, and remains closed over lambing from 1 October to 10 November.

Carpark to Roys Peak 3.5–4 hours

From the carpark the track begins climbing immediately, zigzagging up slopes on the peak's eastern flanks. After about 40–60 minutes, the track reaches the gravesite of Wally Alan Scaife, who owned the Glendhu Station for 50 years. Less energetic walkers may like to turn back here. Beyond, the track sidles and climbs southwards, up another series of zigzags, then to another ascending sidle leading across a tussock basin. The telecommunications tower on Roys Peak is clearly visible above, and it is still as far away as it looks. From the basin to the summit involves another 680 metres of solid climbing.

Over a third stile, the track enters The Stack Conservation Area, which has been retired from pastoral farming. There is a noticeable increase in the health and vitality of

the tussock, and the occasional speargrass makes a prickly appearance too. The track cuts across to the ridge crest, and here the views unfold even more. Mt Aspiring, the only 3000 metre peak south of those in the Mount Cook area, dominates the other mountains, and virtually the whole sprawling extent of Lake Wanaka is visible. For those who are too tired to continue there is no shame in calling it quits here; the views don't get too much better.

More zigzags, and a curl around the back of the peak leads to a final half-kilometre of track up to the summit. Two telecommunications towers are reached first, with the actual trig about 80 metres further on. Those who reach the mountaintop have certainly earned the views, which perhaps even surpass those from Queenstown's Ben Lomond.

Opposite *View over Lake Wanaka and Southern Alps from Roys Peak Track*

Grade Hard

Map F40 Wanaka

Total Walking Time 5.5–7 hours return

Access From Wanaka, take the Wanaka–Mount Aspiring Road for 6 km along the southern shores of Lake Wanaka. The track start is signposted at a carpark, and there is a toilet 2 minutes up the track.

Alternative route Experienced trampers can continue over the top from Roys Peak to Mt Alpha (turning craggy tors here on the western side) on the Skyline Track, which ends down Spotts Creek in the Cardrona Valley. Although poled, much of the route lies on exposed tops, and will require a very full day of some 10–11 hours.

Information DOC Wanaka Tel: 03-443-7660 Email: wanakavc@doc.govt.nz

QUEENSTOWN
BEN LOMOND TRACK

Walkers can be forgiven for thinking they are in the European Alps when they approach this track by gondola, and emerge into a conifer-dominated forest.

Ben Lomond, a significant 1748 metre peak dominating Queenstown, can be approached using the Skyline Gondola, which will save about 400 metres of the ascent. But reaching the peak still requires plenty of good old-fashioned kiwi grunt; even from the top of the gondola it is still a 500 metre ascent to the saddle and another 430 metres to the summit itself.

On a clear day the views are breathtaking; Lake Wakatipu sprawls in its entirety, with Mt Earnslaw prominent near the head. The Remarkables earn their name to the southeast, and the Richardson Mountains offer less familiar profiles to the northwest. Moke Lake is visible below.

This is a serious walk, requiring good fitness and reasonable experience. The track passes almost entirely through exposed, subalpine terrain, and the weather can often be unforgiving. Allow a full day for the climb and the through trip to Arthurs Point. Take plenty of water and food.

Gondola to Ben Lomond Saddle 1.5–2 hours

After exiting the gondola complex, follow paved paths past the luge track, following signs to Ben Lomond. For the first 10 minutes the track passes through a dense stand of douglas firs, the seedlings of which are threatening to overtake the subalpine tops above.

After breaking out onto the tops, the well-benched and graded track reaches a signposted junction where the One Mile Track (which starts from the lakeshore) joins the Ben Lomond Track. Carry on up the track (no marker poles), which has increasingly good views of Lake Wakatipu and the craggy profile of Ben Lomond itself. The track to the Moonlight Valley branches off about 5–10 minutes before the actual saddle at 1316 metres, where there is a bench seat offering a spectacular vista of the complex of mountains in the headwaters of the Shotover Valley.

Ben Lomond Saddle to Ben Lomond Summit 2 hours return

From the saddle to the summit of Ben Lomond (1748 m) is a further 430 metres, following the ridge crest until near the craggy summit, where the trail curls around the back to gain the final few metres. There are occasional cairns but no poles.

Ben Lomond Saddle to Arthurs Point via Moonlight Track 3.5–5 hours

A trail leads from the saddle, less formed but marked with snow poles, crossing several spurs of tawny tussock beneath Bowen Peak. Increasingly good views of Ben Lomond unfold as the track veers north. After about 90 minutes of descent, the track reaches a fence and crosses into the sheep

Moke Lake

Ben Lomond

Moonlight Track

Shady Ck

Shotover River

saddle

Arthurs Point

Ben Lomond Track

Skyline

gondola

One Mile Track

QUEENSTOWN

Lake Wakatipu

N

and cattle country of Ben Lomond Station. Poles lead down towards the Moonlight Valley, skirting patches of briar. At the signposted junction with the Moke Lake track, head right, soon joining a farm road briefly before diverting off onto the Moonlight Track. This track sidles high above the Shotover Gorge through country of broken schist, sheep and briar. Keep a close eye on the main track, for several sheep trails branch off, and they generally offer shortcuts only for four-legged creatures. Before Shady Creek the track rounds a spur to gain a view of Arthurs Point, where more often than not the roar of a Shotover jet boat can be heard. For those without transport here, it is usually easy to hitch-hike the 5 kilometres back to Queenstown.

Opposite Ice formations in Shady Creek

Grade Hard
Map E41 Queenstown
Total Walking Time 5–7 hours for the through trip, plus 2 hours return to the summit.
Access The Skyline Gondola is located at the end of Brecon St, well signposted in the main centre of Queenstown. A re-turn ride costs $20, while a one-way downhill ride costs $10.
Alternative route Ben Lomond Saddle makes a worth-while viewpoint for those without the time or energy to reach the summit. The One Mile Track provides an alterna-tive start and/or descent route for those who prefer not to use the gondola.
Information DOC Queenstown Tel: 03-442-7935

MOUNT ASPIRING NATIONAL PARK
ROUTEBURN FALLS, ROUTEBURN TRACK

The world famous Routeburn Track is justifiably popular for its diverse and often exquisite scenery. While diehards might choose to tackle the entire 32 kilometre track in a single day, most walkers will prefer a shorter portion of the track. Routeburn Falls makes a worthwhile destination and turnaround point. Highlights of the track include stately, moss-draped beech forests, excellent views, and the archetypical Otago burn: turquoise waters and schist-choked gorges. While avalanches can pose problems above Routeburn Falls during winter, the hut is generally an all-season destination. Don't expect solitude!

Routeburn Shelter to Routeburn Flats Hut (20 bunks, wood burner, gas cookers $10/night) 2–2.5 hours

The well-benched and gravelled track begins on the true right of the Route Burn River but crosses almost immediately to the true left on a large footbridge. The track continues through flattish terrain through red beech forest for 30 minutes, crossing two footbridges over side streams. The valley narrows and the track begins a slow climb past a delightful gorge for an hour or so. At the top of the gorge, another footbridge leads back to the true right. A further 25 minutes walking leads to Routeburn Flats Hut, which occupies the edge of a large tussock flat with views into the Route Burn North Branch.

Routeburn Flats to Routeburn Falls Hut (48 bunks, wood burner, gas cookers) 1–1.5 hours

From the flats, an extremely well-graded track leads upwards through increasingly stunted beech forest. The track ascends for 300 metres, crossing two footbridges en route, with the Emily Creek bridge considered about halfway. The large Routeburn Falls Hut lies above the bushline, with grand views over the Routeburn Valley and surrounding mountains. The falls themselves (really a series of cascades over abrupt slopes) are a few minutes walk above the hut.

The turquoise water of the Route Burn on the Routeburn Track

Ocean Peak

Emily Peak

Mt Xenicus

Routeburn Falls Hut

Routeburn Falls

Emily Ck

Routeburn Flats Hut

Routeburn Falls

Routeburn Shelter

to Glenorchy

Routeburn Rd

Route Burn

Lake Sylvan

Dart River

Grade Medium–Hard

Maps E40 Earnslaw, D40 Milford, Mount Aspiring Parkmap

Total Walking Time 6–8 hours return

Access Access is from Glenorchy on the Rees Valley Road, Glenorchy–Routeburn Road and Routeburn–Kinloch Road. Public transport is available to the track from Queenstown or Glenorchy. At the road end is a large carpark with toilets. Nearby is the Routeburn Shelter.

Alternative route Routeburn Flats Hut makes a worthwhile and shorter destination in itself (4–5 hours return).

Information DOC Glenorchy Tel: 03-442-9937
Email: glenorchyvc@doc.govt.nz

Walker at Lake Harris

OTAGO PENINSULA, OTAGO
SANDFLY BAY

The Otago Peninsula forms a long finger that stretches for some 30 kilometres on the southern side of Otago Harbour. It's a place of white sand beaches, redoubtable sea cliffs, and interesting wildlife. A range of walking tracks tempt walkers, but for scenic variety this through track to Sandfly Bay is hard to better. The bay is not named for its voracious insects, but rather the ability of the southerly winds to sweep up sand.

Walkers have a good chance of encountering the rare yellow-eyed penguin and Hooker's sea lion, along with other more common animals such as New Zealand fur seals and variable oystercatchers.

DOC have constructed a wooden hide at the eastern end of Sandfly Bay from which walkers can observe yellow-eyed penguins emerging from the sea at the end of the day. Please respect the penguins by giving them space, and leaving dogs at home.

Walkers of modest fitness and school-age children will enjoy this through walk, which will require some transport juggling.

Sandymount Road to Sandymount via The Chasm and Lovers Leap 1–1.5 hours

From the carpark follow a farm road through a dense boulevard of macrocarpa trees beyond to a farm shed, where the track proper begins. Across a stile, follow poles over grass and tussocks to reach a signposted junction after about 10 minutes. Head left across a second stile to reach the wooden viewing platform at The Chasm after another 5 minutes. The platform provides a vertigo-inducing glimpse into a formidable gulch near the sea edge and a vista of the eastern end of the peninsula. In the other direction are good views of the rugged coastline as far as Harakeke Point, with an impressive sea stack nearby.

Back at the track junction take the track across to a second viewing platform overlooking a natural rock arch, probably a sea cave with a partially collapsed roof, and a basalt cliff known as Lovers Leap.

Beyond this the track leads through tussocks and flax up

Map labels: PORT CHALMERS, Otago Harbour, Portobello, Papanui Inlet, Hoopers Inlet, Highcliff Rd, Sandymount Rd, Seal Point Rd, to Dunedin, Sandfly Bay, Sandymount, Lovers Leap, The Chasm, hide, Sandfly Bay, N

to another track junction near Sandymount. Head right for a 10 minute return trip to the sandy summit (319 m), which is actually the culmination of a giant dune. It has reasonable views with all the landmarks indicated on a plane table.

Sandymount to Sandfly Bay and Seal Point Road
1–1.5 hours

From the junction below Sandymount the track to Sandfly Bay follows an overgrown fenceline through lupins and other vegetation for 10 minutes until emerging onto a sandy gully. Orange marker poles indicate the route through the dunes, an enjoyable downhill romp all the way to where a side track leads to the DOC hide. Look out also for Hooker's sea lions, which have begun to frequent the peninsula more regularly in recent years, but do not approach them closely.

Opposite Sandfly Bay on Otago Peninsula's exposed south coast

From the hide, follow the firm sands near the sea edge along the length of Sandfly Bay to where a route leads steeply up loose sand to a brief section of track and through a gate to end at Seal Point Road.

Grade Easy

Maps I44, J44 Dunedin (note that few of the tracks are indicated on the map)

Total Walking Time 2–3 hours

Access Both Sandymount and Seal Point roads branch off Highcliff Road, which is the main route along the spine of the peninsula. The Seal Point carpark is 16.5 km from the city centre, and Sandymount carpark is 20 km.

Alternative route Sandfly Bay, Sandymount, The Chasm and Lovers Leap all make shorter destinations, but are all worthwhile in their own right.

Information DOC Dunedin Tel: 03-477-9677

FIORDLAND NATIONAL PARK
MILFORD SOUND FORESHORE & BOWEN FALLS

Despite being a place of too many tourists, diesel-belching buses, and rampant commercialism, the grand natural architecture of Milford Sound dwarfs the imprint of humans to such an extent that it commands awe. Maori legend tells of the demi-god Tu-te-Rakiwhanoa, who carved all of Fiordland's 14 fiords with a great digging stick, or ko, and completed Piopiotahi (Milford Sound) last – after he had reached the height of his skill. Legend also has it that the namu (sandfly) was created to protect the beauty of the place: the small, biting insects certainly try their best.

Walkers who carefully plan their visit to Milford for dawn or dusk can escape the masses which descend during the hours straddling midday. The route described is a loop around a point, with good views of Mitre Peak, which connects to the nearby Bowen Falls track using a path around the foreshore.

Suitable for all abilities and ages, the walks can be enjoyed in all weather conditions. Take a coat or umbrella: in sun the views are sublime, in rain the waterfalls are thunderous.

Piopiotahi–Milford Sound Foreshore Walk 20–30 minutes return

From the main Milford Sound carpark, the walk leads through forest near the edge of the sound out to a headland where a seat overlooks tidal mudflats. Most of the walk is either gravel or boardwalks with interpretation panels to explain the area's natural and human history. Although only 1683 metres high, Mitre Peak punches well above its height simply because it spears straight out of the sea. Across Freshwater Basin the Bowen Falls make a fine sight. On a good day Stirling Falls are visible, as well as several formidable peaks including The Lion, The Elephant and glacier-studded Mt Pembroke (2045 m).

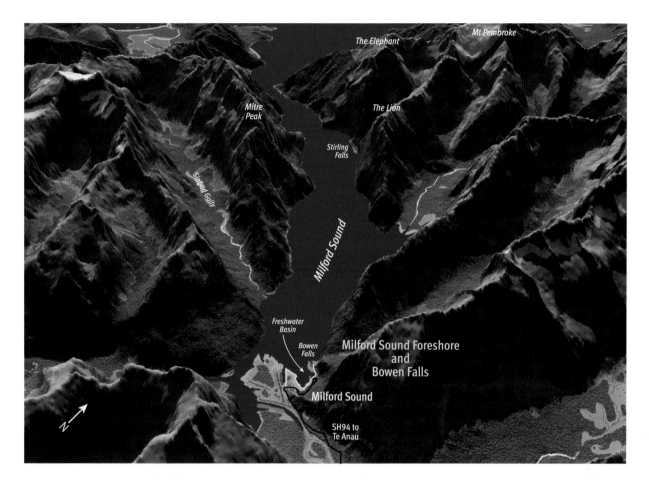

The Elephant · Mt Pembroke · Mitre Peak · The Lion · Stirling Falls · Sinbad Gully · Milford Sound · Freshwater Basin · Bowen Falls · Milford Sound Foreshore and Bowen Falls · Milford Sound · SH94 to Te Anau · N

To Milford Wharves 10 minutes

Back at the carpark, follow the footpath beyond the Milford Hotel, around the foreshore on a covered, boardwalked path that ends at the large visitor centre at the Milford wharves. The Bowen Falls walk begins beyond here.

Bowen Falls 10–15 minutes return

Past the wharves, follow the well-gravelled and easy grade of the Bowen Falls Track to a viewpoint of the 162 metre falls, which tumble from a hanging valley above. After heavy rain, spray from the falls makes them unapproachable to all except those who are prepared for a dousing.

Opposite *Mitre Peak reflected in Milford Sound.*
Photo: Craig Potton

Grade Easy
Maps D40 Milford, Fiordland Parkmap
Total Walking Time 1.5–2 hours return
Access Access is SH 94, 122 km from Te Anau. Allow 2.5 hours for the drive, without stops. The walk begins from the main Milford Sound carpark, on the seaside opposite the Milford Hotel. Public transport is available to the track.
Alternative route The Chasm, a short walk off SH 94 at the Cleddau valley, is very popular but also worth doing (20 minutes return).
Information DOC Te Anau Tel: 03-249-8514
Email fiordlandvc@doc.govt.nz

FIORDLAND NATIONAL PARK
GERTRUDE SADDLE

Even the most cursory glance at the topographical map for Milford will reveal orange contour lines merging into seaweed-like bands: a graphic representation of just how steep the terrain is. Exploiting a small gap in the precipitous walls, the route to Gertrude Saddle offers a rare chance to get amongst the colossal scenery of Fiordland's highest and most heavily glaciated peaks, with a mind-blowing view of Milford Sound. Near the saddle walkers can enjoy a swim in Black Lake, or be simply content to picnic beside its reflections.

During summer, alpine flowers festoon the Gertrude Valley, and near the saddle the rare rock wren can often be seen scampering along the rocks, pausing only briefly to perform its distinctive bobbing dance. This diminutive bird ekes out an existence amongst boulder jumbles above the scrub line, the only truly alpine bird in New Zealand.

Be aware this is a route only, involving a 600 metre ascent on steep and serious terrain, and while marked with cairns it is suitable only for experienced and confident walkers. During winter and early spring the route will require mountaineering skills and equipment, and even then avalanches may well make an attempt too dangerous.

Carpark to Gertrude Saddle 2–3 hours

From the carpark, a fairly worn trail (not marked on the topographical map but lightly marked on the ground) heads upvalley climbing gently through mountain beech before breaking out onto tussock flats. Near the end of the flats the trail heads up the true right of Gertrude Stream beside a spectacular waterfall. About 100 metres above the flats the trail crosses to the true left and picks up a series of cairns marking the climb towards the headwall. The route is now bordered on either side by the imposing walls of Barrier Peak and Mt Talbot. After wet weather, several waterfalls tumble from the surrounding cliffs.

The trail steepens for the last couple of hundred metres to Black Lake and the travel is mainly on rock slabs polished smooth by past glacial action. A cable helps with the last 25 metre haul to the lake and proves particularly useful when the slabs are wet.

Ice can still be seen on the lake right into December, but on hot summer days it is a great place for a swim. From Black Lake another cable leads immediately up a steepish 100 metre climb on rock slabs before sidling across on a rock terrace above the lake (split for much of the year with gentle patches of remnant snow) to a boulder-filled gully. This gully is followed up the remaining 30 minute climb to Gertrude Saddle (1410 m). There at last, stupendous views of Milford Sound and the surrounding mountains unfold. Barrier Knob (1879 m) and Mt Talbot (2105 m) form uneven pommels on either side of the saddle.

Milford
Sound

Cleddau R.

The Twins

Mt Talbot

Gertrude Saddle

Gertrude Saddle
Black Lake

Homer
Tunnel

Barrier Peak

Lake Adelaide

Homer Hut

SH94 to
Te Anau

Grade Hard
Maps D40 Milford, Fiordland Parkmap
Total Walking Time 4–6 hours return
Access The Gertrude Saddle track begins from a carpark 250 metres off SH 94 on the inland side of the Homer Tunnel. Allow 90 minutes to drive the 100 km from Te Anau. Buses and shuttles service the area all year round, except on occasions in winter when the road is closed due to avalanche risk or snowfall. The 30-bunk Homer Hut is managed by the New Zealand Alpine Club (www.alpineclub.org.nz) and is available for overnight stays at $30/night per person. A warden is present during summer months.

Alternative route The one hour walk upvalley to where the terrain steepens will appeal to walkers with less time and experience.
Information DOC Te Anau Tel: 03-249-8514
Email: fiordlandvc@doc.govt.nz

Opposite *Black Lake near Gertrude Saddle. Photo: Rob Brown*

FIORDLAND NATIONAL PARK
KEY SUMMIT, ROUTEBURN TRACK • LAKE MARIAN

KEY SUMMIT, ROUTEBURN TRACK

Set amongst Fiordland's northernmost mountains, Key Summit offers some of the finest views in New Zealand. Accessible off the western part of the Routeburn Track, the Key Summit walk forms a loop around a moor-like mountaintop with tarns and delicate alpine bogs. The topography owes its shape to a great glacier, originating in the Hollyford Valley, that planed over the tops of Key Summit during the last ice age and split into the Eglinton and Greenstone valleys. Nineteenth century surveyors named Key Summit because it forms a divide between three 'key' catchments, each of which flows in a different direction to empty into separate seas: the Hollyford into the Tasman Sea; the Eglinton, a tributary of the Waiau that reaches the Southern Ocean; and the Greenstone, a tributary of the Clutha that issues into the Pacific Ocean. Although not a difficult walk, Key Summit involves a 380 metre ascent, and can be exposed during inclement weather.

The Divide to Key Summit 1.5 hours

From The Divide, the Routeburn Track climbs steadily through moss-laden forest that includes fuchsia and five finger. After about an hour, the track reaches the signposted

Looking out to the Darran Mountains from Key Summit, Fiordland National Park

Mt Gifford

Sabre Peak

Mt Crosscut

Mt Gunn

DARRAN MOUNTAINS

Mt Christina

Mt Lyttle

Lake
Marian

Lake Marian

Hollyford River

Marian Ck

Hollyford River

Lower Hollyford Rd

Routeburn Track

Key Summit

AILSA MOUNTAINS

Key Summit

Howden Hut

Lake
Howden

SH94 to the Eglinton Valley and Te Anau

The Divide

N

turnoff to Key Summit. The Key Summit track zigzags solidly uphill for 20–30 minutes, emerging above the bushline to reach boggy subalpine tops studded by tarns and stunted patches of vegetation. Where the climbing eases, a 30 minute loop track (boardwalked in places) curls around the tops, affording walkers a 360 degree panorama of northern Fiordland. At the southern end of the loop track, a further 15 minute walk leads to an outstanding viewpoint. Here the formidable pyramid of Mt Christina dominates the view westwards, with Lake Marian prominent below and other peaks of the Darran Mountains (Fiordland's highest range) beyond. North and eastwards are the more rounded summits of the Ailsa Mountains, while the Eglinton and Greenstone valleys lie southwest and southeast.

Grade Easy–Medium

Maps D40 Milford, D41 Eglinton, Fiordland Parkmap

Total Walking Time 3 hours return

Access Access is from The Divide on SH 94, 85 km from Te Anau. Public transport is available to the track. At The Divide are a shelter and toilets for use by walkers and trampers.

Alternative route Walkers wanting to stretch their legs might opt to continue along the Routeburn as far as Lake Howden Hut (28 bunks, wood burner, gas cookers), adding 40–60 minutes onto the trip.

Information DOC Te Anau Tel: 03-249-8514
Email: fiordlandvc@doc.govt.nz

LAKE MARIAN, FIORDLAND NATIONAL PARK

During the last ice age, which ended some 14,000 years ago, much of northern Fiordland was covered by great glaciers, the remnants of which still perch on the higher parts of the Darran Mountains. After the ice retreated, many lakes formed from meltwater that filled the glacier-carved depressions. Lake Marian is a superb example of a cirque lake, scooped out of the head of a Fiordland valley by a tributary ice-flow of the main Hollyford Glacier. Surrounded by precipitous mountains it is both a beautiful and formidable place.

Most Fiordland side streams, including Marian Creek, follow a typical 'hanging valley' pattern. Arising in steep mountains as a series of waterfalls, the streams flow through a flat section of valley, often occupied by a lake. Then the streams thunder through a gorge, losing height rapidly before merging with the river in the main valley. Walkers can expect a well-marked and formed tramping track, with one stream crossing, and a substantial but not overly arduous ascent.

The Ailsa Mountains seen from Key Summit

Hollyford Road Carpark to Lake Marian
1.5–2 hours

The Lake Marian Track begins beside the sizeable Hollyford River, which is crossed on a footbridge. The first section is a well-formed and gravelled track, which follows the Hollyford River downstream for 5 minutes through luxuriantly mossy forest before heading up the Marian Valley. After 10–15 minutes it reaches a wooden gantry offering good views over the boisterous cascades of the Marian Creek.

Shortly beyond, the route becomes a typical tramping track, rocky and rooty in places, and begins a 400 metre climb up beside Marian Creek through silver beech forest with the occasional Fuchsia and patch of mountain ribbonwood. The track fords one small side stream en route, which may be impassable after heavy rain. After the track levels out somewhat, the track surmounts an old (now forested) moraine wall: the dam behind which Lake Marian formed. The track ends abruptly near the lake's rocky edge, above

which Mts Lyttle, Christina and Crosscut rise severely, with waterfalls streaming from innumerable bluffs.

Grade Medium
Maps D40 Milford, D41 Eglinton, Fiordland Parkmap
Total Walking Time 3–3.5 hours return
Access The start of the Lake Marian Track is 1 km along the Lower Hollyford Road, which branches off SH 94, 90 km from Te Anau. Allow about 90 minutes for the drive. There are toilets at the carpark.
Information DOC Te Anau Tel: 03-249-8514
Email: fiordlandvc@doc.govt.nz

Above *Wooden gantry above Marian Creek, Lake Marian Walkway.*

FIORDLAND NATIONAL PARK
SHALLOW BAY

Manapouri is New Zealand's second deepest lake, fifth largest, and arguably the most beautiful. The lake has an intricate, forested shoreline, with 34 islands, and a backdrop of formidable mountains.

The 60 kilometre Kepler Track, one of DOC's Great Walks, forms a circuit between the southernmost arm of Lake Te Anau and the northern reaches of Lake Manapouri, near the township of Te Anau. Walkers can enjoy a section of the track by following the portion that leads to Shallow Bay, one of the more delightful of Lake Manapouri's many beaches.

The small Shallow Bay Hut offers walkers respite from the elements or sandflies (which can be downright predatory), and during summer the lake has good swimming. On flat, easy, forested terrain this track suits walkers of most abilities and will appeal to families with school-age children.

Rainbow Reach to Shallow Bay Hut (6 bunks, open fire, $5/night) 1.5 hours

From Rainbow Reach the track immediately crosses a substantial footbridge over the Waiau River to reach the main Kepler Track. Head left along the true right bank, passing through mature beech forest cloaked in vibrant moss. After 25–30 minutes the track bends westwards, crosses Forest Burn on a footbridge, then – after a further 25–30 minutes – reaches the edge of a sizeable wetland. A worthwhile side track (5 minutes return) leads to a viewing platform on the edge of a small lake in the wetland, which reflects the nearby mountains on a calm day.

The main track soon crosses a boardwalk over an arm of the wetland, and about 15 minutes later reaches the signposted Shallow Bay turnoff. Here walkers divert off the

main Kepler Track (which continues on for 25 minutes to Moturau Hut) to reach Shallow Bay on the shores of Lake Manapouri.

Follow the shoreline for 10–15 minutes past a camping area and toilet, and around one promontory, to reach Shallow Bay Hut, set just back from the beach (don't be tempted by a track marked by a large orange triangle which heads inland). From a promontory just past the hut, Rona and Buncrana islands make picturesque scenes across the lake surface, particularly at dawn or dusk.

Opposite *Dawn, Shallow Bay, Lake Manapouri with the Kepler Mountains behind*

Grade Easy

Maps D43 Te Anau, Kepler Trackmap, Fiordland Parkmap

Total Walking Time 3 hours return

Access The turnoff to Rainbow Reach is 12 km south of Te Anau on SH 95. The carpark is a further 1.5 km along a gravel road, where there is a nearby toilet, water supply and shelter. During summer shuttles service Rainbow Reach.

Alternative route Walkers wanting a longer walk can return to Te Anau on foot, using the section of the Kepler Track between Rainbow Reach and the control gates of Lake Te Anau. This largely follows the Waiau River through stately beech forest. Allow an extra 2.5–3.5 hours.

Information DOC Te Anau Tel: 03-249-8514 Email: fiordlandvc@doc.govt.nz

THE CATLINS, SOUTH OTAGO
NUGGET POINT, CANNIBAL BAY, PURAKAUNUI FALLS •
CATLINS RIVER WALK, CATLINS FOREST PARK

NUGGET POINT, CANNIBAL BAY, PURAKAUNUI FALLS

While scenic in places, the South Island's east coast is largely devoid of truly wild and natural coastlines. The notable exception is the Catlins, which straddles the border between Otago and Southland. At first glance, the sombre forests of the Catlins look like a piece of the West Coast that has been uplifted and dumped on the east coast. But closer inspection will reveal a very distinctive part of New Zealand, one of simple cribs (elsewhere in the country known as baches), of rare wildlife (including yellow-eyed penguin, Hooker's sea lions and even the occasional sea elephant) and of fierce seas and untamed coastlines.

The many scenic and scientific reserves spanning the Catlins offer a multitude of walks, which are rarely any longer than an hour or two. For this reason, three walks feature here, each of which displays a different aspect of the area: the craggy headland and lighthouse at Nugget Point; the wildlife and sands of Cannibal Bay; and the lush forest and attractive cascades of Purakaunui Falls. Taken together these walks could occupy a pleasant day and will suit walkers and families of all abilities.

Nugget Point 20 minutes return

From the carpark, the well-benched and gravelled track leads above coastal cliffs and wind-rattled flax to the narrow crest of this impressive headland and beyond to a lighthouse (10 minutes one way). Adjacent to the lighthouse is a viewing platform with an excellent outlook over the myriad rock stacks offshore. After a southerly blow, crashing waves make the air heavy with spume.

Another worthwhile stroll is the short track leading down to a yellow-eyed penguin hide at Roaring Bay, which is accessible off The Nuggets Road near Nugget Point (allow 20 minutes return). Best time to visit is at dusk, when the penguins are returning from a day spent feeding at sea.

Access: On The Nuggets Road, some 10 kilometres southeast of Kaka Point and 30 kilometres from Balclutha.

Cannibal–Surat Bay 1–2 hours return

Prominent New Zealand geologist James Hector named Cannibal Bay after the discovery of human bones amongst the dunes, but he made an incorrect assumption – the area was a Maori burial ground, not the scene of a grisly feast. From the road end it is a 5 minute walk out to the sandy beach, a favourite haunt of Hooker's sea lions. Take care to give these large creatures plenty of room.

Stroll southwards along the beach for 30 minutes or so, then follow a marked track that crosses through dunes on an isthmus beside False Islet. Surat Bay lies at the broad mouth of the Catlins River. Walkers with suitable transport

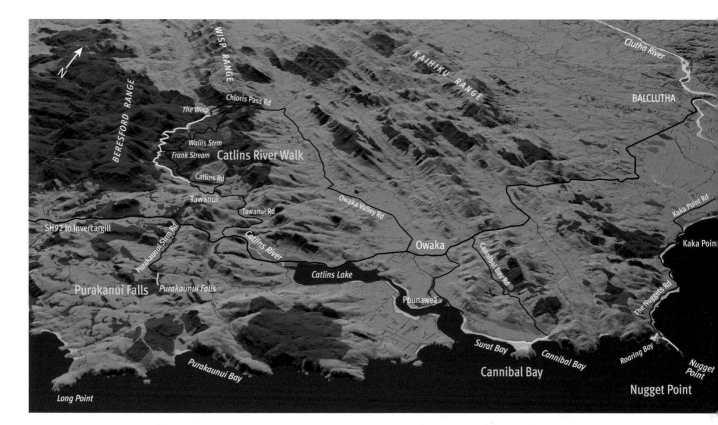

arrangements can walk the length of Surat Bay to Duttons Road (allow 2–3 hours for the through trip).

Access: Some 3 kilometres north of Owaka on SH 92, turn off onto Cannibal Bay Road and follow the gravel road for 8 kilometres to the signposted carpark.

Purakaunui Falls 20–25 minutes return

One of the Catlins most popular walks, this easy track leads to the attractive cascading Purakaunui Falls. The well-benched and gravelled track leads through lush podocarp–beech forest beside the Purakaunui River to reach a lookout over the falls (this first section is suitable for wheelchairs). Beyond, a steeper, rougher track descends to a second viewpoint at the base of the falls.

Access: Turn off SH 92 at a junction 13 kilometres west of Owaka onto Purakanui Falls Road and follow this for 5 kilometres to the large carpark which has a picnic area and toilets.

Grade Easy (all three walks)

Maps Maps showing the walk locations, available from the Catlins Information Centre, are more useful than topographical maps.

Access The Catlins is accessible on SH 92, which connects Balclutha with Invercargill. The main service town is Owaka (32 km south of Balclutha), which has accommodation, petrol, a store and a visitor centre.

Alternative route Other worthwhile walks include Lake Wilkie, Jack's Blowhole, Matai Falls, McLean Falls, Curio Bay and Cathedral Caves.

Information DOC Otago Tel: 03-477-0677, Catlins Information Centre, Owaka Tel: 03-415-8371, Email: info@catlins-nz.com, www.southernscenicroute.co.nz

Opposite *Purakaunui Falls, Catlins Forest Park*

CATLINS RIVER WALK, CATLINS FOREST PARK

The Catlins River winds a sinuous path through the silver beech forests of the Catlins Forest Park. It's a delightful river, one that flows strongly but slowly, with occasional picturesque cascades over small drops.

Transport arrangements are required for those who want to complete the whole through trip; otherwise walkers can tackle one or more of the shorter sections both ways. The top half of the river is the more scenic, as the lower half passes beside some sections of plantation pine forest.

Be careful to stay on the main track, as DOC has pest control tracks in the area to protect a local population of the endangered yellowhead or mohua. The main track is pretty obvious, although largely unmarked except for the occasional permolat.

The track will suit walkers of moderate fitness; but be aware there are four swingbridges with quite steep approaches to negotiate.

The Wisp to Wallis Stream 60–75 minutes

From the road end the track enters a short area of fir plantation on the true left of the Catlins River before reaching the first swingbridge after 10 minutes. Now on the true right, the track wends through mossy silver beech forest, passing some delightful cascades in the river. After a further 40 minutes the track crosses the second swingbridge and passes an elongated forested island around which the Catlins River divides. The Wallis Stream picnic area is set in a small clearing just before a signposted track junction where it is possible to exit out to Pukepiko Road.

Wallis Stream to Frank Stream 1–1.5 hours

The main river trail continues downstream on the true left, soon passing a three-wire bridge (don't cross here, this is for DOC staff only). After about 30–40 minutes of delightful riverside walking, the track climbs briefly over a small promontory to reach the river again at the third swingbridge. More riverside walking ensues, perhaps the most delightful of the whole track. In one place the entire Catlins River surges over a sloping cascade, with upstream trees arcing their limbs from bank to bank as if to reach each other. The track crosses the fourth and last swingbridge shortly before meeting the Frank Stream junction, where the Frank Stream Track exits to the Main Catlins Road.

Walkers observe a Hooker's sea lion, Cannibal Bay

Frank Stream to Tawanui 2–2.5 hours

Beyond the Frank Stream Track junction the main track continues down the true left of the Catlins River, at first in native forest but soon passing through an area of pine forest. A muddy section of track climbs across a milled area, before the track again enters a section of beech trees. The last stretch has pine forest on the track side, with views across the river to where there is farmland. At Tawanui there is a grassy camping site, toilets and a water tap.

Above *The Catlins River winding through the predominantly silver beech forest of Catlins Forest Park*

Grade Easy–Medium
Map G46 Clinton
Total Walking Time 4–5 hours
Access From the main Catlins town of Owaka, take the Owaka Valley Road for 20 km (most of it gravel), then turn off onto the Chloris Pass. Another 5 km leads to The Wisp carpark. The Tawanui camping area is 11 km on gravel roads from SH 92, 10 km west of Owaka. Owaka Motors offers a drop-off for $20 per head, Tel 03-415-8179.
Alternative route Any one of the above three sections can be completed separately.
Information DOC Otago Tel: 03-477-0677

RAKIURA NATIONAL PARK, STEWART ISLAND
MAORI BEACH • ULVA ISLAND, PATERSON INLET

MAORI BEACH

When it was created in 2002, Rakiura National Park became New Zealand's fourteenth national park. Stewart Island is the smallest of New Zealand's three main islands and the 140,000 hectare park encompasses about 83 per cent of the island.

The 2–3 day Rakiura Track, one of DOC's Great Walks, is an easy 29 kilometre loop from the island's only town Oban (more commonly referred to as Halfmoon Bay). Walkers wanting a shorter taste of the track will enjoy the trip to Maori Beach, on the first part of the circuit.

The track begins from Lee Bay, where a large stylised anchor chain marks the official entrance to Rakiura National Park. Unless suitable transport arrangements have been made, walkers will have an additional stroll – scenic but undemanding – along the road between Oban and Lee Bay (allow about 1.5 hours each way). The track standard is high, mostly benched or boardwalked with little mud.

Lee Bay to Maori Beach 1.5 hours

From Lee Bay the track crosses forested terrain, mostly near

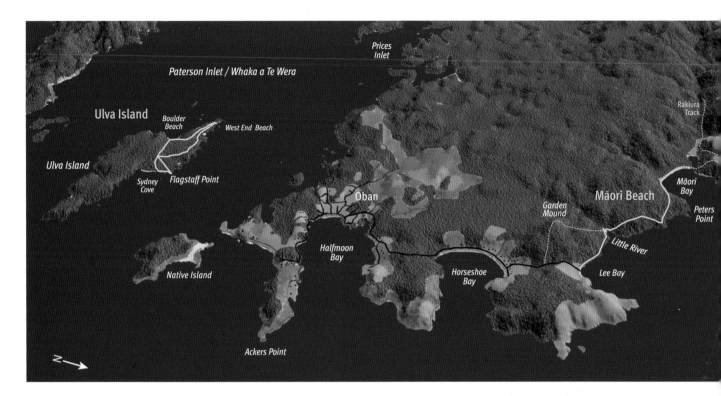

the shore, until it emerges at the western end of the bay to reach a footbridge over the Little River estuary, near a former sawmilling site. Here, the Garden Mound track branches off (a possible return route that climbs over a forested hill with a good viewpoint).

Either cross the Little River estuary on a footbridge, or at low tide walk across the sand, to pick up the track on the far side. The track wends inland for a brief period, before descending to near the coast, around the Peters Point headland and down towards Maori Beach. At low tide cross straight onto the eastern reach of the beach, otherwise use a muddy high-tide track to access the western end of the bay.

During the years 1913–1931 a large sawmill operated at Maori Beach, where timber, (mainly rimu) was cut over about an 800 hectare area. Walkers can still observe a large boiler and steam engine on site, and wonder how a small community, including a school, once existed here. When operations ceased, it ended Stewart Island's sawmilling era.

Grade Medium

Maps E48 Halfmoon Bay, Rakiura Parkmap

Total Walking Time 6–7 hours return (including travel on roads from Oban)

Access Transport to Halfmoon Bay from Invercargill is via either ferry or plane. Oban offers accommodation, cafés, a store, and a DOC visitor centre. The track to Maori Beach is accessible on Horseshoe Bay and Lee Bay roads, about 4.5 km from Oban.

Alternative route A shorter loop track is possible over Garden Mound from Lee Bay (4–5 hours return, including walking time on roads).

Information DOC Rakiura Tel: 03-219-0002, Email: stewartislandfc@doc.govt.nz

Opposite *Crown fern* Blechnum discolor *and* rimu Dacrydium cupressinum *trunk, Ulva Island, Paterson Inlet. Photo: Rob Brown*

ULVA ISLAND, PATERSON INLET

Most people who visit Stewart Island notice that birdlife there is markedly better than on mainland New Zealand: hearing kaka, kakariki or even witnessing a kiwi are not unusual events on Rakiura, thanks to an absence of mammalian predators like stoats, ferrets and weasels. But even on Rakiura, birdlife is compromised by the presence of other pest mammals, including rats.

Ulva Island, an open sanctuary in Paterson Inlet, remains free of these pests, thanks to a successful DOC rat eradication programme in the mid-1990s. Since 2000 several endangered birds – saddleback (tieke), yellowhead (mohua), Stewart Island robin and fernbird (matata) – have been reintroduced to the island.

Several operators based at Oban run tours or water taxi services across to Ulva Island, where walkers have a number of tracks to choose from. The loop track described below links several beaches on the 267 hectare island, including Sydney Cove, Boulder Beach and West End Beach. It crosses the island on good tracks through dense forest dominated by rimu, southern rata and kamahi.

Walkers disembark onto the island at a wharf near Flagstaff Point. A nearby historic post office, now over 130 years old, became Rakiura's first post office in 1872. It was situated in the store of Charles Traill, who also commissioned a cutter – named Ulva – to be built on the island. For several years the Ulva ran weekly sailings to and from the mainland carrying stores, passengers and mail. The post office continued to operate until 1923, by which time it had become something of a tourist attraction – helped no doubt by the entirely incorrect reputation it earned as the most southerly in the world. Although situated on a small area of private land on the island, walkers can still see it behind some houses.

Another thrill of visiting Ulva Island is the chance to see captive kakapo. For a brief period each year DOC has kakapo available for viewing, providing the best opportunity the public has to see these extremely rare parrots.

Please help ensure the ongoing rat-free status of the island by checking your bags for rodents before leaving Oban.

Decaying tree after kaka have removed grubs, Ulva Island Photo: Rob Brown

Flagstaff Point to Sydney Cove, Boulder Beach and West End Beach 60–75 minutes

From Flagstaff Point follow the well-graded trail for 5 minutes to Sydney Cove, where there is a picnic area and shelter. About halfway down Sydney Cove, the track heads inland, gently climbing across the backbone of the island through dense podocarp–hardwood forest to reach a sign-posted track junction. Take the track that leads on a gentle descent to Boulder Beach, reached about 30 minutes after departing Sydney Cove. At the north end of the beach the track heads inland again, striking westwards to reach West End Beach after a further 25 minutes.

West End Beach to Flagstaff Point 60–75 minutes

From West End Beach the track once again climbs gradually onto the island's crest, back to the track junction. Here, take the track that leads directly to Flagstaff Point.

Grade Easy

Maps E48 Halfmoon Bay, Rakiura Parkmap

Total Walking Time 2–2.5 hours

Access Transport to Oban from Invercargill is by ferry or plane. Oban offers accommodation, cafés, a store, and a DOC visitor centre. Access to Ulva Island is possible by arranging a tour or water taxi, or by hiring sea kayaks.

Alternative route Several shorter loops can easily be undertaken: for example from Sydney Cove to Boulder Beach and return. Flagstaff Walk is a short 20 minute loop to the point where, during the days of the post office, a raised flag indicated the arrival of mail to 'mainland' Stewart Islanders.

Information DOC Rakiura Tel: 03-219-0002

Email: stewartislandfc@doc.govt.nz

Photographing weka, Ulva Island. Photo: Rob Brown

REFERENCES AND FURTHER READING

Barnett, S. & Brown, R. *Classic Tramping in New Zealand* (Nelson: Craig Potton Publishing, 1999)

Barnett, S. *North Island Weekend Tramps* (Nelson: Craig Potton Publishing, revised edition 2004)

Barnett, S. Smith, R. *Tramping in New Zealand, 40 Great New Zealand Tramping Trips* (Nelson: Craig Potton Publishing, 2006)

Brailsford, B. *Greenstone Trails, The Maori and Pounamu,* (Hamilton: Stone-print Press, second edition 1996)

Brown, R. *Rakiura, The Wilderness of Stewart Island* (Nelson: Craig Potton Publishing, 2006)

Brown, R. 'A Heart for the Hills', in *New* Zealand *Geographic* No. 60, November–December 2002 pages 79-95

Dawson, J. & Lucas, R. *Nature Guide to the New Zealand Forest*, (Auckland: Godwit, 2000)

Dennis, A. *A Park for All Seasons, The Story of Abel Tasman National Park*

Department of Conservation, Arthur's Pass National Park Management Plan (Christchurch: Department of Conservation, 2006, draft)

Greenaway, R. *The Restless Land – Stories of Tongariro National Park* (Turangi: DoC/Tongariro Natural History Society, 1998)

Groves, N. *South Island Weekend Tramps* (Nelson: Craig Potton Publishing, 2003)

Latham, D. *The Golden Reefs, An Account of the Great Days of Quartz-Mining at Reefton, Waiuta and the Lyell* (Nelson: Nikau Press, second edition 1994)

Hall-Jones, J. *Stewart Island Explored*, (Invercargill: Craig Printing Co., 1994)

Host, E. *Thomas Brunner, His Life and Journeys* (Nelson: Nikau Press, 2006)

Maclean, C. *Kapiti* (Wellington: Whitcombe Press, 1999)

Maclean, C. *Tararua – The Story of a Mountain Range* (Wellington: Whitcombe Press, 1994)

Molloy, L & Smith, R. *Landforms, The Shaping of New Zealand* (Nelson: Craig Potton Publishing, 2002)

Moore, P. & Ritchie, N. *Coromandel Gold* (Palmerston North: Dunmore Press, 1996)

Ombler, K. *Ruahine Forest Park, A Guide to Family Walks, Tramping Tracks and Routes* (Nelson: Craig Potton Publishing, 1993)

Ombler, K *National Parks and Other Wild Places of New Zealand* (Cape Town: Struik New Holland Publishers, 2001)

Ombler, K. *A Visitor's Guide to New Zealand National Parks* (Auckland: New Holland, 2005)

Potton, C. *Classic Walks of New Zealand* (Nelson: Craig Potton Publishing, 1997)

Reed, A.H. *First Walks in New Zealand* (Auckland: Reed, 2007)

Shaw, Derek *Northwest Nelson Tramping Guide* (Nelson: Nikau Press, 1991)

Solnit, R. *Wanderlust, A History of Walking* (New York: Viking, 2000)

Thornton, J. *The Reed Field Guide to New Zealand Geology* (Auckland: Reed, new edition 2003)

Wilson, K-J. *Flight of the Huia* (Christchurch: Canterbury University Press 2004)

Wright, J. *Tramping in South Island Forest Parks* (Auckland: Heinemann-Reed 1990)

NZ Wilderness is a monthly magazine that regularly features articles on tramping, conservation, mountain biking, sea kayaking, climbing and natural history www.wildernessmag.com.

Check out the Federated Mountain Clubs (FMC) website: www.fmc.org.nz for a list of tramping and climbing clubs in New Zealand.

OTHER BOOKS OF INTEREST

Classic Tramping
in New Zealand
SHAUN BARNETT &
ROB BROWN

Travelling in
New Zealand
SIMON HENSHAW

BIRD'S EYE GUIDES

South Island
Weekend Tramps
NICK GROVES

North Island
Weekend Tramps
SHAUN BARNETT

Tramping in
New Zealand
SHAUN BARNETT

BIRD'S EYE GUIDES

Classic Walks of
New Zealand
CRAIG POTTON